GLOBAL HISTORY OF THE PRESENT
Series editor | Nicholas Guyatt

In the Global History of the Present series, historians address the upheavals in world history since 1989, as we have lurched from the Cold War to the War on Terror. Each book considers the unique story of an individual country or region, refuting grandiose claims of 'the end of history', and linking local narratives to international developments.

Lively and accessible, these books are ideal introductions to the contemporary politics and history of a diverse range of countries. By bringing a historical perspective to recent debates and events, from democracy and terrorism to nationalism and globalization, the series challenges assumptions about the past and the present.

Published

Thabit A. J. Abdullah, *Dictatorship, Imperialism and Chaos: Iraq since 1989*

Timothy Cheek, *Living with Freedom: China since 1989*

Alexander Dawson, *First World Dreams: Mexico since 1989*

Padraic Kenney, *The Burdens of Freedom: Eastern Europe since 1989*

Stephen Lovell, *Destination in Doubt: Russia since 1989*

Alejandra Bronfman, *On the Move: The Caribbean since 1989*

Forthcoming

James D. Le Sueur, *Between Terror and Democracy: Algeria since 1989*

Mark LeVine, *Impossible Peace: Israel/Palestine since 1989*

Hyung Gu Lynn, *Bipolar Orders: The Two Koreas since 1989*

Nivedita Menon and Aditya Nigam, *Power and Contestation: India since 1989*

Helena Pohlandt-McCormick, *What Have We Done? South Africa since 1989*

Nicholas Guyatt is assistant professor of history at Simon Fraser University in Canada.

About the author

Alejandra Bronfman taught at the University of Florida and Yale University before moving to the University of British Columbia, where she is associate professor in the Department of History. She has traveled extensively in the Caribbean, and has published widely on the region; her books include *Measures of Equality: Social Science, Citizenship and Race in Cuba, 1902–1940* (2004).

About this book

The Caribbean stands out in the popular imagination as a "place without history," a place which has somehow eluded modernity. Haiti is envisioned as being trapped in an endless cycle of violence and instability, Cuba as being in a 1950s timewarp; the Jamaicans are ganja-smoking Rastafarians, while numerous pristine, anonymous islands are simply peaceful idylls. The notion of "getting away from it all" lures countless visitors, offering the possibility of total disconnect for the world-weary.

In *On the Move* Alejandra Bronfman argues that in fact the opposite is true: the Caribbean is, and has always been, deeply engaged with the wider world. From drugs and tourism to international political struggles, these islands form an integral part of world history and of the present, and are themselves in a constant state of economic and social flux in the face of global transformations.

On the Move: The Caribbean since 1989

Alejandra Bronfman

Fernwood Publishing
HALIFAX | WINNIPEG

Zed Books
LONDON | NEW YORK

On the Move: The Caribbean since 1989 was first published in 2007

Published in Canada by Fernwood Publishing Ltd, 32 Oceanvista Lane, Site 2A, Box 5, Black Point, Nova Scotia B0J 1B0

<www.fernwoodpublishing.ca>

Published in the rest of the world by Zed Books Ltd, 7 Cynthia Street, London N1 9JF, UK and Room 400, 175 Fifth Avenue, New York, NY 10010, USA

<www.zedbooks.co.uk>

Cover designed by Andrew Corbett
Set in Arnhem and Futura Bold by Ewan Smith, London
Index: <ed.emery@thefreeuniversity.net>
Printed and bound in Malta by Gutenberg Press Ltd

Distributed in the USA exclusively by Palgrave Macmillan, a division of St Martin's Press, LLC, 175 Fifth Avenue, New York, NY 10010.

A catalogue record for this book is available from the British Library.
US CIP data are available from the Library of Congress.

Library and Archives Canada Cataloguing in Publication:
Bronfman, Alejandra, 1962-
    On the move : the Caribbean since 1989 / Alejandra Bronfman.
(Global history of the present)
Includes bibliographical references and index.
ISBN 978-1-55266-243-4
    1. Caribbean Area--History--1945-. 2. Caribbean Area--Civilization--20th century. I. Title. II. Series.
F2183.B76 2007   972.905'2   C2007-903324-5

ISBN   978 1 84277 766 4 hb
ISBN   978 1 84277 767 1 pb
ISBN   978 1 55266 243 4 (Fernwood Publishing)

Contents

Acknowledgments

In writing this book I have incurred sizable debts to the librarians and archivists who have supplied many of the materials I used. Some aspects of this book rest on the work of many scholars of the Caribbean. It has been a privilege to draw from such a rich, exciting field of inquiry. Closer to home, many people have assisted me in several stages of this book. My research assistants, Kate Mooney, Pau Milán, and Darcy Gaechter, deserve the most profuse expressions of gratitude. They contributed with a great deal of intellectual energy as well as painstaking research. The students on my courses on Caribbean history deserve thanks for allowing me to use them as sounding boards as I rehearsed some of these claims on them.

I have benefited from conversations about structure and content with Alexander Dawson, and admired the example he set as a writer. My colleague Steven Lee was very helpful at some key moments of conceptualization, as were Courtney Booker and Christina Lupton, whose interest in narrative fed my own. Many thanks must go to Nicholas Guyatt, who talked me into it, Anna Hardman, who saw me through the initial stages, and Ellen McKinlay, who patiently led me to the end. I am grateful also to the anonymous reader, who provided sharp insight. Allen Sinel improved this book immeasurably – it would have been impossible without him. And finally, thanks to Maia Q. Dawson, who teaches me, and to the marvelous Peter Hirschfeld, for more than I can say.

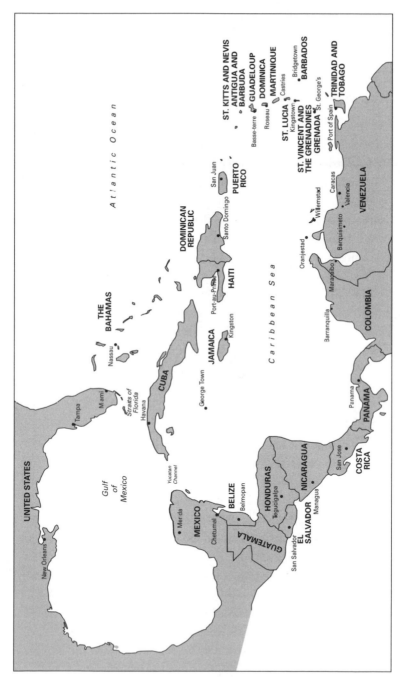

The Caribbean Basin

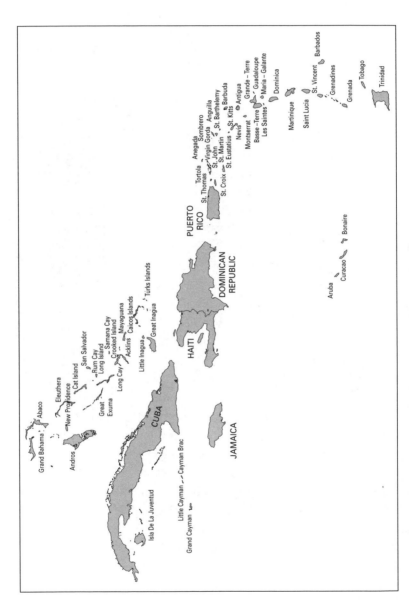

Greater and Lesser Antilles

Introduction

The Caribbean's allure comes in part from the idea that it is a place where one can escape from the wider world. A photograph of a perfect beach suggests that time has stood still. History has not swept through the place with buildings or roads or even people. The beach will remain unchanged, the photograph suggests. It beckons with an invocation of timelessness. Yet this imagining of the Caribbean as timeless idyll has a dystopic counterpart. If one idea of the Caribbean holds out the promise of a pristine island offering the world-weary the possibility of total disconnect from their harried lives, another set of imaginings envisions a series of nations left behind, incapable of overcoming the violence and corruption brought on by legacies of slavery and colonialism. In this version the accompanying photograph would be of a corpse in the street, shot and abandoned by a society so stunted that it cannot even attend to its dead. In both cases, the Caribbean has somehow stepped out of time and into the purity or hopelessness that characterizes its essence. But as soon as one sets the photographs aside and takes a closer look, the notions of timelessness and isolation fall apart. These images of impermeable paradise or vulnerable volatility arose only as a result of long histories of contact with faraway places. The circulation, of people, commodities, capital, and information, has shaped Caribbean economies, politics, and cultures from the earliest moments of colonization. As anthropologist Sidney Mintz observed, "Caribbean people have always been entangled with the wider world."[1] This book will, following Mintz and others, use that entanglement as a point of departure and explore the ways in which recent global transformations have reconfigured Caribbean societies, economies, and cultures.

Defining the Caribbean is not an easy task. One of the more difficult aspects of writing about the Caribbean as a unit is its dazzling variety. It is a region colonized by at least five European powers, founded by immigrants from Africa, Europe, and Asia who encountered traces of Amerindian life, and decolonized in fits and starts over the course of the nineteenth and twentieth centuries (and in some cases not at all). It has developed political systems ranging from parliamentary democracies to lengthy dictatorships leaning both right and left. Its heterogeneity cannot be overstated. Fragmentation has been one of the principal metaphors used to describe the place. At the same time, as many have observed, shared histories of colonialism, dependence on export-based economies, and cultural invention resonate across the islands. The tension between consistency and fragmentation makes understanding the Caribbean a fascinating challenge.

Geographically, the Caribbean can mean a number of things. The Caribbean sea both separates and unites a series of islands, most commonly divided up into the Greater Antilles, which includes the larger islands of Cuba, Hispaniola, and Jamaica, as well as the Bahamas and Turks and Caicos, and the Lesser Antilles, made up of numerous smaller islands and island nations such as Guadeloupe, Martinique, and former British colonies like Antigua, Barbuda, and St Lucia. Puerto Rico floats in between these two groups, while Aruba, Curaçao, and Bonaire hug the coast of Venezuela, much farther south. The notion of the Caribbean Basin demarcates a larger region that includes Guyana, French Guyana, Suriname, and Belize, as well as the coasts of Venezuela and Colombia, where residents tend to claim Caribbean identities. The islands' diverse vegetation and topography include mountainous regions and plains, tropical jungle, and arid, rocky landscapes. Much of the land is devoted to the farming of sugar, bananas, coffee, and citrus. The beaches and coral reefs for which the Caribbean is so well known are no invention; they exist in abundance.

The populations of the islands are not particularly large. On the high end of the spectrum is Cuba with 11 million people. Haiti and the Dominican Republic, which share the island of Hispaniola, each have about 9 million inhabitants. (Haiti, about half the size of the Dominican Republic, has a very high population density.) Of the smaller islands, Aruba has 101,000 people, while 13,000 people live on tiny Anguilla.[2] Despite these relatively small numbers, the population is extraordinarily diverse. The islands are home to people of African, European, South Asian, Chinese, and Middle Eastern descent. They practice Christianity, Islam, Judaism, Buddhism, and many variants of African-derived religious systems. Their official languages are English, Spanish, French, and various Creole languages. The legacies of slavery and migration have produced complex systems of racial categories and racial identities. Each island has developed its particular way of classifying the combinations of physical features, class statuses, and location that have come to define "race." While in Haiti many residents proudly claim African ancestry, in the neighboring Dominican Republic those with similar family histories will deny that they are "black." Some nations have sought to unify their people by creating inclusive racial categories like "mulatto," "mestizo," or "Creole" in reference to the products of African and European sexual unions. Others, like Trinidad and Tobago, emphasize the heterogeneity of their populations with terms like "Callaloo nation," meant to celebrate the coexistence of people of African, European, Indian, Amerindian, and Chinese descent.

A very brief history

Amerindians living in the Caribbean experienced European colonization only briefly before they were almost entirely decimated by disease and overwork. When Columbus arrived in the fifteenth century he was in search of other things, and although he founded Santo Domingo on the island of Hispaniola, the Spanish soon moved on to the mainland. The Caribbean remained on the margins of European colonizing efforts until the English and French discovered the profitability of sugar. In the seventeenth and eighteenth centuries sugar was the source of a great deal of wealth and the cause of a demographic transformation. The millions of slaves from Africa would become the majority on several islands, bringing with them religions, languages, institutions, and agricultural practices that changed the Caribbean in countless ways. Sugar dominated the economies even after slave systems began to fall apart, beginning in Haiti, where slaves were freed after a protracted struggle for independence between 1791 and 1804. Slave emancipation was a long process, beginning with Haiti and ending with the abolition of slavery in Cuba in 1886, involving a complicated combination of slaves' efforts to obtain freedom and political conflicts among the elite over the moral and economic viability of the system.

In the twentieth century, former Spanish colonies experienced divergent trajectories. While Cuba moved through a period of liberal democracy to socialist revolution, the Dominican Republic experienced thirty years of right-wing dictatorship followed by stable electoral politics. But the United States entered the picture in both of these places, with capital for investing in sugar, bananas, and railroads and with military interventions to ensure the protection of those interests. Puerto Rico remained in limbo as it became first a United States colony and then a commonwealth, where its residents are US citizens who cannot vote in federal elections and are regarded as immigrants when they move to the mainland. For the most part, French and British colonies remained attached to their metropoles in the early part of the century. Growing anti-colonial and nationalist movements that began in the 1920s gained momentum, especially by the end of World War II, culminating in a wave of independence in Jamaica, Trinidad, Guyana, and other islands. When Trinidad discovered significant oil reserves its economy surged ahead of the other former colonies'. But they all shared degrees of infrastructural neglect and social and ethnic tension. Meanwhile, the French islands remained officially regions of France as *départements*, with benefits from state subsidies and privileges as part of the French state. Although there is not space here for a full accounting of each island and its trajectory, this very brief sketch should serve to underscore the diversity of experience as well as the ways in which the Caribbean continues to be shaped by deep political, economic, and cultural ties to former or present colonizers. At the same time, its inhabitants have been resourceful and inventive in finding ways to navigate their particular combination of isolation and forced reliance on external markets for economic survival.

Two simple arguments have shaped this book. The first is that the Caribbean is not a place out of time or without history. To the contrary, it is very much a participant in historical change and has always been so. Moreover, it is not the passive recipient of outside forces but has acted to shape its history. As a producer of sugar and consumer of coerced labor, as a locus of imperial rivalry and revolution, this region has never stood outside the networks and flows that defined modernity. The foundational plantation economies connected the Caribbean to financial markets and changing consumer practices. The production of sugar depended on the technology of travel and of industrialized agricultural production. In the eighteenth and nineteenth centuries, Caribbeans participated in the intellectual and political revolutions that elevated claims about equality and freedom above entrenched invocations of tradition and privilege. The island nations produced bananas and consumed baseball (and then produced it again), witnessed streams of emigration and received countless visitors, and jostled for position, along with other small countries, when superpowers attempted to divide up the world. More recently, reverberations from the collapsed Soviet Union, the integration of global markets, and transformations in information and communication technologies have provided the impetus for the Caribbean to keep changing. This book will challenge stereotypical notions of Caribbean "timelessness" by looking at the ways in which ordinary people have negotiated political instability, economic devastation, and the uneven attentions of US policy-makers in the past twenty years.

The second argument is that the circulation of commodities is one of the unifying aspects of Caribbean history. All islands are shaped by things that circulate, and more so in the recent past, when aspects of globalization have made it easier for things to circulate at greater quantities and greater speed. Despite obvious differences in political organization, and failed attempts at economic integration, strategies for survival have come to depend on linkages within and beyond the Caribbean, thus reconstituting a region – heterogeneous, unequal and ambiguously bounded, to be sure – profoundly embedded in global processes. Globalization has not just happened to the Caribbean. The Caribbean has participated in the making of globalization.

The last twenty years have seen a deepening engagement with Europe, Latin America, and the United States. The dismantling of communism in the Soviet Union and eastern Europe has affected the story insofar as it resulted in a more widespread acceptance of free market ideologies. In the late 1980s Latin America and the Caribbean were emerging from a series of economic crises driven by ballooning debt. Gradually islands gave up on social democratic experiments and replaced them with cutbacks in social spending demanded by neoliberal tenets. As state interventions shrank, Caribbeans looked for alternative strategies for survival, ranging from emigration to attracting foreign investment. Just as important, if not more so, was the greater volume and speed with which capital, information, goods, and people began to move. These changes did not circumvent the Caribbean; they affected it deeply. More precisely, it was the combined acceleration of flows and the widespread adoption of neoliberal policies which drove the new degree of engagement with the global economy. At the same time, these have taken shape with distinctly local inflections.

This is not a comprehensive study of the Caribbean over the last twenty years. Rather I use the space available to tell a series of stories that are particularly revealing of one important aspect of recent change. This book will look at four things that circulate: people, capital, drugs, and information. To be sure, a unifying theme risks running rampant over the peculiar specificities of place. What I want to point to here is the tension between the specific and the general, crucial to understanding the Caribbean. There are many ways to solve this problem of narrative. By looking closely at particular examples I can trace change over time and look at some of the nuances and unevenness in the way these circulations work. The cases I have chosen are extreme and paradoxical, but the circulations define these places in important ways. For reasons outlined below, in three cases the focus will remain a single island, while for the final case I have broadened the geographic scope to emphasize the unevenness of globalization.

Circulations

People In the Caribbean, very little of what existed before European colonization survives. The few Amerindians who witnessed the arrival of the Europeans did not fare well. Although their exact fates are the subject of some dispute, most historians agree that all but a very few were eliminated within the first few decades of European contact. This set the stage for waves of migration both free and coerced. People came from Africa, England, France, Spain, and Holland, first; later they came from India and China, and even later from Lebanon, Syria, Greece, and Germany, among others. People arrived and never left, or arrived and returned home, or circulated among the islands. Laborers traveled from island to island looking for work, administrators traveled back and forth from the metropoles to the islands while wealthier landowners oversaw their operations from afar. Emigration began to occur in earnest after World War II, as West Indians sought employment and education in Europe, Puerto Ricans were lured to the mainland by a burgeoning manufacturing sector in New York, and Cubans fled Castro's expropriations and political whims. Spurred by the introduction of air travel, the lure of jobs or education, people began to travel. Migration was not necessarily permanent but rather involved circular patterns of leaving and returning. People went off to work and then went home, repeating that pattern year after year. Others remained abroad but left their families at home, creating single-parent households that benefited from two incomes. Remittances grew as proportions of incomes, and have become among the most significant contributors to Caribbean economies today. For many islands, the numbers of those abroad equal the numbers of those who remain on the island. For many of those abroad, being away is not a permanent state but rather part of a strategy of circulation, intended to maximize incomes for emigrants and their families. This means that Caribbeans have adjusted their careers, languages, and habits according to the host country. But they have also re-created some aspects of community and culture in cities like New York, Montreal, London, Paris, and Miami, where you can eat curried goat or *tostones*, listen to radio broadcasts in Haitian Creole, or participate in a rally for an upcoming election in the Dominican Republic.

Capital Capital from outside the Caribbean has been a key aspect of its history. Since the islands were colonized for primary resource export, they developed deep dependencies on foreign capital and food imports which continue in varying degrees. A colonial legacy meant that profits more likely returned to the metropole rather than remaining in place. Structurally this began with sugar, since it required industrialized processing on location. The capital and goods for building sugar factories, where sugar cane was turned into processed sugar, were the first in what would become a succession of flows of foreign capital. Efforts in the 1940s and 1950s to move away from overdependence on primary exports and turn to manufacturing proved disappointing. In the late 1970s Caribbean countries struggled with mounting debt. Attempts to liberalize economies in places like Jamaica and Guyana resulted in economic hardship for those less well off as the government was unable to maintain social and economic infrastructures. As trade in traditional agricultural commodities has become less and less lucrative, many Caribbean nations have begun to search for alternatives. They have turned increasingly to the service sector, including tourism, data processing, and communications technologies. This has involved an increase in direct foreign investment. After a relatively restrictive phase in the 1960s and 1970s in which trade was more closely controlled by the state, the Caribbean has opened the door to foreign capital in unprecedented ways.

Contraband Illicit flows of all kinds have been part of the Caribbean's history. Goods have circulated to the region, from the region, and through the region. Initially, efforts by European powers to control commerce gave rise to many attempts to evade those controls. From the sixteenth century, when the Spanish Crown tried to control all commerce flowing from the Caribbean to Europe by limiting commercial activity to a few ports, smugglers avoiding duties and taxes began a lively trade in numerous goods. One of the main smuggled goods was leather, a much sought-after commodity produced from the cattle that came to populate the islands. Contraband tobacco also made its way from the Americas, principally the coast of Venezuela, to Europe. Slaves were smuggled into many of the islands regularly during the seventeenth and eighteenth centuries, as slavers took advantage of the numerous coves and tiny bays to evade competitors and customs houses. When the Spanish finally followed the lead of other European nations and abolished their slave trade in 1850, the flourishing slave society in Cuba continued to receive slaves illicitly for another twenty-five years.

Later, proximity to the United States as one of the major consumers of illicit goods gave the Caribbean an advantage as a transshipment point. US prohibition, in the 1920s, sent many Americans to the Caribbean, particularly Cuba, in search of liquor and other forbidden pleasures. As tourism burgeoned in the 1940s and 1950s, the trade in illicit drugs grew alongside it. Cuban traffickers began to handle heroin, marijuana, and cocaine, retaining some of it for domestic markets and circulating the rest to the north. In the last twenty years the flow of Jamaican marijuana, most prevalent during the 1970s, has been replaced by cocaine, which has begun once again to move through the Caribbean as a result of complex interactions among producers in Latin America and North American enforcement efforts. The expanding levels of consumption of marijuana and especially cocaine in the 1980s and 1990s drew the Caribbean in as part of a commodity trade worth billions of dollars. Between 60 per cent and 80 per cent of the cocaine entering the United States passes through the Caribbean. Interlocking parts of the drug trade came together to produce a complex structure of interdependent drug trafficking and drug interdiction.

Information If goods and people circulate, information must accompany them. The Caribbean has taken part in the radical transformations in communications technologies throughout the twentieth century. As the United Fruit Company developed radio technology immediately following World War I in order to administer its expanding Caribbean ventures, the region witnessed an earlier and more widespread acquisition of radio than other parts of the Americas. When United Fruit installed two-way radio communications connecting its ships to its land-based operations, they created an infrastructure that facilitated the adoption of radio broadcasting. In Cuba, for example, the first broadcast was heard in 1922, only two years after the inaugural US broadcast in Pittsburgh in 1920. At the same time, communications gave Caribbeans the means through which to imagine themselves as part of a far-reaching, if vaguely defined, region. Residents of Barranquilla, on the Colombian coast, would be more likely to listen to Cuban broadcasts than to those emanating from Bogotá, the capital city. As a medium that crossed national boundaries and did not require literacy, radio brought the outside world into homes, schools, and public spaces in a way previously unimaginable.

But radio access was uneven, and while on some islands nearly all inhabitants could listen to a radio by the 1940s, on others that became true only in the 1960s. Telephone service has never been evenly or well distributed. For precisely this reason the most recent changes in telecommunications that allow one to bypass telephone lines altogether are important. The cost of a telephone call is much lower than it was in the 1970s. The spread of cellular phones in places like Jamaica, Guyana, and Suriname has been quite dramatic. Computers, fax machines and Internet connections are less expensive and more widely available. New developments including fiber optics cable and wireless technologies have begun to change the way Caribbeans live their lives, do their jobs, and engage in family and social relationships.

At the same time, the Caribbean is still divided up into the anglophone, francophone, and Hispanic islands whose residents probably have closer ties to Europe or North America than they do to neighboring islands. There is no newspaper published in the Caribbean that circulates throughout the whole region. The closest thing to a regional newspaper is the *Miami Herald*, which does circulate in three languages. While previously only the print edition was available, now it is accessible online.

The increased flow of information has generated both enthusiasm and dismay. Some argue that access to information will facilitate the provision of social services and education and encourage a more participatory society. Others see in its uneven distribution the exacerbation of current social and economic inequalities and the reproduction of distance among cultures. Some welcome the ready availability of music, videos, and diverse other entertainments, while others worry about the survival of the local in the face of widely disseminated popular culture. These debates continue discussions initiated in the early stages of radio broadcasting. But they have taken on a new urgency as the pace of distributing telecommunications and information technology has accelerated. They are vital discussions in the Caribbean today.

The chapters

Haitians who leave The chapter on the circulation of people looks at Haiti. By 1989 Haiti was in the midst of one of the most important transitions of its history. Twenty-nine years under the authoritarian rule of François and Jean-Claude Duvalier had come to an end three years earlier. After years of grim stability, Haitians were engaged in deep conflicts over who was to rule and how politics would be conducted. When people left the country in response to these conditions, they did not sever their ties but rather found ways to wield influence or alleviate hardship from afar. The combination of volatile politics and great inequality has placed Haitians at an extreme end of one of the most common strategies of Caribbean people: leaving with the intention of maintaining contact and contributing back home. They have been at the forefront of the invention of transnational citizenship.

Cubans and capital When the Soviet Union fell and its subsidies disappeared, Cuba, for many years isolated from global capitalism and pressures to conform to neoliberal demands, found itself in a position that demanded change. And change it did. The way Cuba opened to market economies and sustained socialism is one of the fascinating stories of the last twenty years. Cuba has stepped up its participation in activities deemed central to the globalized economy: tourism, exploitation of resources, and foreign investment. In doing so it has begun to look more like the rest of the Caribbean. What makes the case so interesting is that it has done so while upholding some defining aspects of its revolution: commitments to education and healthcare and, perhaps most important, a lively anti-imperialist stance.

The nationalist critiques of US imperialism that defined the revolution fifty years ago continue to be the most powerful argument for Cubans to remain loyal to their regime. The added twist is that this now resonates in Latin America and the Caribbean in more powerful ways than ever. Emerging from years of right-wing dictatorships, Latin Americans from Venezuela to Argentina, Brazil, Chile, and Bolivia have claimed Cuba as inspiration as they turn to the left.

Jamaica's lucrative trade Jamaica occupies a unique place in the history of illicit flows because both marijuana and cocaine move in and out of the island. Historically, countries or regions that produced drugs were not necessarily the principal consumers, and traditionally one substance dominated the traffic. In Jamaica marijuana is produced for both consumption and export, while cocaine is not produced and consumed only in insignificant quantities there. Yet a growing proportion of the cocaine that enters the United States and the United Kingdom passes through Jamaica. By looking at Jamaica it is possible to see how these two flows have been interrelated and how they are distinct. It also affords an opportunity to understand the different meanings these substances take on in local contexts. Jamaica was hit particularly hard in the 1980s as a result of debt burdens, liberalization policies that resulted in high levels of unemployment, and falling bauxite prices in the midst of a search for revenue. Many Jamaicans were particularly susceptible to the appeal of the drug trade as a source of income.

Electronic revolutions The final chapter will expand its geographic scope to encompass several islands. Changes in communications technology have resulted in a number of new developments throughout the region. The chapter will focus on three particularly transformative processes: the introduction of cellular telephones, the adoption of the Internet, and the proliferation of offshore gambling sites. It will look across the region as a way to get at how these have, or have not, effected a "digital divide," creating new kinds of inequalities based on access to technologies. It will also examine the extent to which communications technologies have shaped understandings of the Caribbean as a unified region rather than a series of isolated islands.

Conclusion The book ends with an exploration of one of the liveliest conversations in the Caribbean today: the struggles over historical memory. The final chapter will briefly revisit the previous chapters but then circle back to the study's starting point with a critical exploration of specific ways in which Caribbeans have understood their own relationship to the past and to recent transformations. In 1989 many residents of the Caribbean were more engaged in debates about the meaning of Columbus's arrival five hundred years earlier than in speculations about the future of communism and the cold war. Global processes in the past seemed much more definitive to their identities than those of the immediate present. On the islands, schizophrenic preparations involved the clean-up and restoration of the sites of Columbus's arrival accompanied by growing protests about the celebratory nature of the commemorations. Groups claiming to represent the indigenous peoples of the Caribbean cried genocide and brutality while governments arranged for the arrival of the replicas of Columbus's ships, the *Niña*, the *Pinta* and the *Santa María,* and hoped for accompanying tourist dollars.

One of the more spectacular efforts was the construction of a lighthouse in Santo Domingo, in the Dominican Republic. This enormous structure, shaped like a cross and standing ten stories high on a base, intended as a monument to Columbus that would eventually house his remains, incited more conflict than celebration. Critics focused on the cost, which they claimed was $70 million, far exceeding the government's claim of $11 million. They also protested the removal of thousands of people from the site in preparation for building. But most importantly they objected to the commemoration of a man who could be said to have initiated the destruction of indigenous civilizations on the island. What was intended to prop up the faltering regime of Joaquín Balaguer, the octogenarian in his sixth term as president, ended up embarrassing him. His plans for the visiting Pope to hold a mass to be held at the base of the lighthouse led to three weeks of anti-lighthouse demonstrations. Some heads of state, including King Juan Carlos of Spain, refused to attend. This was one of the more dramatic conflicts over historical memory and commemoration, but hardly the only one. Caribbeans are engaged in a complex dialogue over the meaning of their past and how it relates to remaking the present.

1 | Transporting citizenship

By January 1986, Jean-Claude Duvalier's days were numbered. Although his pudgy cheeks and youth had earned him the nickname Baby Doc, the brutality of his rule, the antithesis of childlike innocence, contributed greatly to his downfall. In 1970, Jean-Claude had been named to succeed his father François, who had been "president for life" since 1957. After François (known as Papa Doc) died the following year, Jean-Claude ruled for another fifteen years until 1986, when in the face of political disarray and popular discontent he boarded an airplane for France, where he still resides. The combined Duvalier regime is remembered by many as a devastating and cruel era, one in which a small, corrupt elite clung to their wealth and power while most Haitians fought against extreme poverty and tried to shield themselves from the violence of the notorious *Tonton Macoutes*, Duvalier's private, brutal police force.

Baby Doc left under inauspicious circumstances. Although he tried to leave surreptitiously, the entire city of Port-au-Prince knew that the airplane that took off at 4 a.m. on 7 February 1986 was his. And they started to celebrate. These celebrations spread quickly to Miami, New York, Montreal, and Boston, where thousands of Haitians had been glued to their radios. They spread more slowly to the rest of Haiti, where communications were less instantaneous. In France, where Baby Doc, his wife Michèle Bennet, and a party of twenty-two others were headed, government officials gritted their teeth and announced that he would be allowed to remain only for eight days.

The former dictator's fortunes crumbled as thoroughly as his legitimacy. He first took up residence in a luxury hotel, a converted monastery near Grenoble. When he arrived, he owned two apartments in Paris and a chateau just outside the city. He and his family lived in a villa in Mougins, near Cannes. Since he owned property in

France, officials were forced to allow him to remain there. Initially, he and his wife allegedly spent $168,780 a month on clothing and indulged themselves with baubles such as a $68,500 clock. Several attempts by Haitians to track down and recover the money he was believed to have embezzled led to revelations of extravagant spending but nothing else. Eventually, however, he lost everything; he and his wife divorced in 1993 and she is thought to have kept most of the assets, although the details have never been clear. As of 2003 Jeane-Claude Duvalier resided in a one-bedroom apartment in Paris. The rent, $1,000 a month, was paid by a friend of his girlfriend.

This story begins at the end of this era, when Baby Doc became, if the most notorious, only one of millions of Haitians abroad. Over the next twenty years a succession of military governments and democratic regimes, along with continuous pressure for neoliberal reforms on the part of international aid institutions, both drove Haitians away from the island and made them determined to participate in events from afar. As new emigrants joined established communities abroad and the state abdicated its role as provider of social services, the nature of the Haitian diaspora changed. In the process Haitians expanded and changed the meaning of citizenship: they became transnational citizens. Some observers claim that up to 2 million Haitians, or one-quarter of the entire population, reside abroad, in Canada, the United States, France, and on various Caribbean islands, as well as the neighboring Dominican Republic. In their transnational condition they reflect and reproduce the inequalities that characterized their lives at home. While wealthy emigrants have been enormously influential in domestic politics, acting as proxies for the state in the provision of social services, and wielding power and money in electoral politics, poorer emigrants in search of work cross the Dominican border on an almost daily basis, struggling to take advantage of wage differentials whenever possible. Opposition groups huddle abroad and plan their next seizure of power. The history of the past twenty years cannot be told without attending to those Haitians who have left. Before proceeding to their stories, it may be useful to give a brief account of Haiti's history and post-Duvalier politics.

Haiti was once the wealthiest of the French Antillean colonies, producing more sugar during the eighteenth century than any of the other European possessions. But sugar was produced on the backs of slaves, who at the height of sugar production constituted the majority of the population. A slave revolt in 1791 in the midst of the upheaval precipitated by the French Revolution was followed by a series of struggles and reversals on the island of Hispaniola, the outcome of which was an independent Haiti and the emancipation of its slaves. Suddenly it was the poorest country rather than the wealthiest colony, as much of the sugar production halted, diplomatic recognition by the United States and Europe took years to materialize, and the French demanded reparations for property destroyed during the war.

During the nineteenth century, the country was relatively prosperous, and flexed its muscles with an invasion of neighboring Santo Domingo. Divisions between Haitians who identified as black and those who identified as mulatto continued to shape the political sphere. Mulatto elites tended to control Port-au-Prince and the southern part of the country, while black elites who tended to think of themselves as representing the peasant majority centered their power in the rural areas and the north. Fierce competition over domination of state machinery facilitated the involvement of the United States, as each side invited foreign intervention as a way to further weaken their opponents.

A US occupation between 1915 and 1934 expanded the military and made it a feasible route for upward mobility. In addition, it briefly united the upper classes against the American presence. But it also tightened the financial relationship as the USA controlled the revenues from the customs houses even after they terminated the occupation. The rest of the twentieth century, until 1986, was shaped by the Duvalier regime.

Haiti shares the history of US presence followed by a dictatorship with other Caribbean countries, including the Dominican Republic, Nicaragua, and Cuba. In all these places, US occupations bolstered military institutions and created the trappings of modernization, including roads, schools, and sanitation. The dictators rose up through the military ranks and stepped into positions in which their power depended in part on maintaining high levels of patronage already set in the days of the US occupations. Throughout the cold war they were useful allies, with Anastasio Somoza of Nicaragua, Rafael Trujillo in the Dominican Republic and Duvalier staking anti-communist territory for long periods, while Cuba's Fulgencio Batista did so more briefly, until forces led by Castro ran him out of the country.

The Duvalier regime has been variously described as populist, kleptocratic, autocratic, and tyrannical. Haitian anthropologist Michel-Rolph Trouillot has written about Duvalier's Haiti as a place where the state and the nation stood far apart from one another.[1] A rapacious state divested the nation of its wealth and felt no compunction or duty to redistribute that wealth. It was a place where an elite few enjoyed enormous privilege at the expense of the vast majority of the poor. The Duvaliers had created a system whereby a handful of families controlled both political offices and state-run enterprises. The industries, such as cement, flour, sugar, and cooking oil, were not efficient, but somehow the families reaped profits. Tax rates were very high, but they targeted the struggling peasantry. Rumors of embezzlement and siphoning off funds begin with the Duvaliers and extend to the elite sector. The large bureaucracy supported what there was of a middle class, a source of loyalty or vulnerability for the regime, depending on its ability to offer living wages. Among the beneficiaries of the state were the *Tonton Macoutes*, which Duvalier had founded in order to counteract the police force in place and create an apparatus for support and legitimization of his regime. They terrorized the population with violence and repression. The poor had few options. One of the strategies that financial institutions had encouraged Duvalier to follow was to keep wages low and attract overseas operations. Although in the 1970s some experiments with manufacturing yielded positive results and a measure of prosperity, they proved impossible to sustain in a meaningful way. When Haitians found factory work, they discovered that they could not live solely off their wages. Agricultural workers did not fare much better: land distribution was badly skewed, and deforestation and erosion a constant and insurmountable problem. The underpinnings of Duvalier's rule were a virulent anti-communism, which ensured US support, and the total absence of democratic institutions, which, combined with swift and effective repression of opposition, kept him in place until he was able to name Jean-Claude as his successor.

By 1986, however, the Duvaliers were gone. The aftermath was dominated by the meteoric career of Father Jean-Bertrand Aristide, the former priest who entered the political arena not long before Baby Doc left. With his charismatic personality and blistering sermons criticizing the establishment and the status quo, he had gathered widespread support among poor Haitians and aroused the hostility of the elite. For many, a mass conducted in 1985 was the catalyst for the strikes and protests that eventually brought Baby Doc down. By 1989 Aristide's church had been attacked and torched, and he had been ordered out of the country by the nation's bishops, but his supporters had fought successfully to allow him to remain. A year later he was elected president with 60 per cent of the popular vote. Haitians expected enormous changes. The many Haitians who had left over the years watched from abroad and shared those expectations. But his populist outlook and left-leaning policies were too much for a conservative elite with ties to the military, who ousted him seven months later. After three years of exile he was returned to power in 1994 with the assistance of a United States-backed invasion. He served out his term until 1996 when his ally in the Lavalas party and former prime minister René Préval was elected president.

Aristide was re-elected in 2000 (Haitian law forbids consecutive terms as president but allows re-election), demonstrating Haiti's capacity for electoral politics and peaceful transfers of power. But a bitter opposition had formed against him, including former members of the military, which Aristide had disbanded in 1994, Duvalier loyalists, and others generally threatened by his vows to work for the poor. At the same time, the United States had suspended a $500 million aid package in the light of allegations of electoral wrongdoing in the May 2000 parliamentary elections. Aristide apparently sought to address these allegations by suggesting that the senators occupying the contested seats resign, but the USA and international financial institutions continued to withhold aid. In this context the economy was put in an even more precarious situation than ever, as unemployment soared, and the government found itself unable to provide potable water for millions of Haitians or respond to the growing AIDS epidemic. Material discontent was matched by political discontent as Haitians became disillusioned with Aristide, who seemed more intent on attacking his political enemies than in remedying social issues. The opposition, many of whom had gathered across the border in the Dominican Republic, grew increasingly bold, and in late 2003 they marched into Haiti and created a crisis that forced Aristide to leave the country again in February 2004. The interim government ruled without legitimacy in Haiti and abroad, and eventually yielded its power in the elections of early 2006 that placed René Préval at the head of government for a second time, while Aristide joined the ranks of exiles observing from afar.

Early migrations

Haitians have been migrating to the United States for hundreds of years. Many fled to the United States during the upheaval of the late-eighteenth-century revolution that culminated in the abolition of slavery and the island's independence in 1804. The majority of these were wealthy slaveowners, mostly white and some mulatto, who took their slaves with them. In the United States they settled along the east coast, with concentrations in Baltimore, Philadelphia, Charleston, and especially New Orleans. Successive waves of migration took place over the course of the nineteenth century. Haitians established their presence in the United States in various ways. Wealthier Haitians integrated themselves into elite social circles, nuns opened convents, and tradespeople plied their crafts. The wave of migration that followed the Haitian revolution not only increased the numbers of free people of color in many US cities; it also added numerous skilled workers, including masons, carpenters, nurses, and tailors. Some eventually became politically active as well. One of the most influential was Rodolphe Desdunes, whose struggles against racial discrimination led to his involvement in the 1894 Supreme Court case Plessy v. Ferguson, the source of the "separate but equal" justification for racial segregation. Rodolphe was an activist and essayist whose Haitian father had come to the United States just before Rodolphe was born. A freemason living in New Orleans, Desdunes challenged the Separate Car Act of 1890, which had legislated separate railroad accommodations for blacks and whites. His colleague and neighbor Homer Plessy subsequently took up the challenge in the famous case against Judge Ferguson in 1894.

During the first US occupation of Haiti (1915–34) the country witnessed a reverse sort of migration: American marines, missionaries, teachers, and anthropologists travelled to Haiti and came back with more knowledge and a mix of fascination and fear of the place. During this period, a rising demand for labor in the Caribbean drove circular migrations, as Haitians left their homes to work on the Panama Canal, on many United Fruit Company banana plantations scattered throughout the region, or in the cane fields in Cuba or the Dominican Republic. This was seasonal labor, and many Haitians fell into a pattern of leaving and returning, year after year. These workers chased wages wherever they might be available.

When François Duvalier's regime began in 1956, discontented or dissident middle- and upper-class Haitians began to leave as well, their departure facilitated by American policies. President Kennedy encouraged those opposed to Duvalier's regime to come to the United States. While the initial wave comprised mostly elite Haitians, the black middle class followed, starting in the 1960s. In 1965, a US immigration act permitted family members to bring close relatives, and many Haitians did so. By the late 1960s 7,000 Haitians had become permanent immigrants, and another 20,000 came with temporary visas.

While President Kennedy had encouraged and welcomed those escaping Duvalier's dictatorship, President Johnson was not so welcoming and developed stronger ties with Duvalier, who shared his hostility to revolutionary Cuba. His efforts to curb immigration only led to an increase in illegal entry, and those Haitians who came to be known as "boat people" began arriving in the late 1960s. With fewer choices about where to land, these people crowded into Miami. Class differences in Haiti continued to be relevant in the United States, as wealthier immigrants put off by the segregationist South tended to settle in northern urban centers like New York, Boston, and Chicago, or French-speaking Montreal, while poorer Haitians had little choice but to stay in Miami once they arrived there.

Debates in the United States over the status of Haitian migrants revealed Americans' deep ambivalence about migration. While some welcomed arriving Haitians, others made it as difficult as possible for them to stay. These conflicts were inevitably entangled with racial issues. Initially, undocumented Haitians were jailed. While their defenders saw them as refugees, their jailers said they were merely illegals. After becoming president in 1977, Jimmy Carter made it easier for Haitians to claim refugee status and thus facilitated the entry of many Haitians. Yet this created political problems for the president as Florida's politicians attacked these new policies. The Immigration and Naturalization Service weighed in on the side of the Florida politicians and their anti-immigrant constituencies. It devised a program that sent Haitians who arrived without documentation back to Haiti, made it nearly impossible for them to claim refugee status, and denied them access to lawyers. In the early 1980s the combined forces of anti-immigration sentiment, pro-Duvalier policies promulgated by Ronald Reagan, and the unrelated but immediately relevant Mariel crisis (which brought thousands of Cubans to the USA and particularly to Miami) worked to reduce legal immigration from Haiti to the United States to a trickle.

Politicization and recognition

For those Haitians who had left, however, the late 1980s proved pivotal. Developments both in Haiti and in the United States politicized them in unprecedented ways. Despite a long-standing reluctance to make public declarations on Duvalierist politics, the joyous celebrations that erupted in New York, Miami, and Boston upon news of Baby Doc's departure suggest that many Haitians were paying close attention to the dictator's fate. This burst of energy from the spontaneous celebrations crystallized around several issues in the early 1990s as Haitians' political mobilization became more overt.

Many remember the AIDS march in April 1990 as a moment when thousands of Haitians came together in shared concern over their misrepresentation in the American media and health systems. But they also remember it as one of a very few moments when expressions of solidarity cut across deep and continuing divisions among Haitians abroad. In Brooklyn, Washington, and Miami, and in front of the US embassy in Port-au-Prince, Haitians protested the US Food and Drug Administration's ban on Haitians donating blood, because of their alleged propensity to carry the HIV virus. Newspaper estimates of the numbers of protesters ranged from 50,000 up to 85,000.[2] Whatever the numbers, this moment was a clear expression of both anger over stigmatization of being Haitian in the United States and a belief that the voicing of discontent would precipitate a response by the authorities. By all accounts this was a forceful, boisterous occasion, as marchers crossed the Brooklyn Bridge into Manhattan, ending up in front of City Hall. The success of this organizing effort was due not only to the perceived urgency of the issue, but also to increasingly efficient tactical organization.

Aristide recognized this energy and potential to influence US policy soon after his election in late 1990 when he formally called on the tenth department to participate in his vision of a new Haiti. Haiti itself is divided into nine administrative units called departments, and the tenth department included all Haitians living abroad. Although the 1987 constitution barred Haitians abroad from voting, Aristide knew they wielded influence in other ways. Wealthy Haitians abroad contributed large sums to the campaigns of both Aristide and Marc Bazin in 1990, also offering technical expertise and other resources. It was Haitians in the United States who wrote speeches and created ads during these campaigns. They also raised up to $250,000 to fund new government projects. Over the years many Haitians in the USA had become quite adept at lobbying for Haiti's interests, which would prove useful during the period of Aristide's first exile. Haitians abroad also worked informally with their friends and neighbors who remained in Haiti, advising many of them how to vote, and making sure that they did. Three of the major newspapers representing widely disparate political stances were founded and continue to be published in the United States: *Haiti Observateur*, *Haiti Progrès*, and *Haiti en Marche*.

Aristide's formal recognition of the role of Haitians overseas emboldened this already easily mobilized population. Enormous crowds of 150,000 to 200,000 again marched over the Brooklyn Bridge in October 1991, just days after the coup, calling for his return. In the aftermath of the coup, once the USA imposed an embargo on the military regime, connections between supporters of Aristide in

Haiti and abroad became even tighter. Aristide supporters in Haiti were able to maintain contact with members of the diaspora, relaying information about post-coup conditions and keeping abreast of the situation abroad. Evading the reach of the military government, correspondents in hiding in Haiti were able to broadcast directly to Haitian programs in New York, Miami, and Boston.[3]

At the same time, Aristide's overthrow precipitated the departure of thousands of Haitians, who, struggling with changing economic circumstances and fearing for their futures after the loss of the politician they perceived as their protector, saw migration as their best option. During the first few months after the coup, estimated numbers of Haitians leaving, mostly in small boats, heading for south Florida, reached 38,000. At first, the United States was determined to send them back to Haiti, but policies shifted over the next few years. The USA began to use Guantánamo naval base as a temporary holding pen, where Haitians could apply for asylum. Initially higher numbers than usual were granted asylum, but later the majority were turned away and repatriated.

In this uncertain political and economic atmosphere, wealthier Haitians also took flight, and could do so more easily, integrating into sizable communities of middle- or upper-class Haitians in North America. Although many of those prosperous Haitians became part of American or Canadian society, they maintained or even strengthened their ties to Haiti. In part, their access to resources in North America afforded them the means with which to do so.

Both the more established groups and the newly arrived depended on the broadcasts of Haitian radio stations in New York for news and as a tool for further political mobilization. Radio became an important political tool in Duvalier's final days, as well-known broadcasters like Jean Dominique of Radio Inter fed oppositional sentiment with his scathing critiques of the regime in Haitian Creole.[4] Haitians in the USA made the radio an even more crucial aspect of their lives as transnational citizens, as it created and strengthened ties among Haitians in New York as well as between Haitians abroad and Haitians in Haiti. Very often news broadcast in New York came from telephone communication with people still in Haiti. When the forces in opposition to Aristide approached Port-au-Prince in the months before his second departure in 2004, Haitians in New York knew what was happening almost as soon as Haitians at home did. When rebels took the city of Gonaïves as part of their approach to the capital, that news reached Radio Soleil, one of the most popular Haitian stations in New York, within hours, via phone calls from Haiti. Since journalism on the ground could be dangerous, and major news agencies seldom focus on Haiti, this type of transmission may well have been the speediest possible.

Radio Soleil has been operating in Brooklyn for many years and has weathered many crises. Founded by Ricot Dupuy, it has come to occupy an important place in the lives of Haitians in New York. Dupuy came to New York when he was nineteen and set up Radio Soleil in 1993, though he had run Haitian news programs on community radio stations for many years. Once on the air, the station provided Haitians with news tailored to their interests, as conceived by Dupuy. He began to scan British, French, and American newspapers and share relevant stories in Creole. But the station was not just a news source. Dupuy encouraged people to come by with announcements for him to read on the air. He gave away special receivers needed to hear the broadcasts. Haitians began to drop by the station to discuss the news, or just chat. Dupuy was also called upon to mediate disputes or locate social services or assistance for those less familiar with the city.

Even as political mobilization became more active and overt, it exacerbated divisions among Haitians, both at home and abroad. The very administration of the tenth department caused friction among groups of Haitians in the United States. Aristide established a central committee to coordinate this department, which would be divided, as others in Haiti were, into *arrondissements*. The committee selected a leader for each region, but in many instances these leaders lacked legitimacy in their constituencies since they were not locally elected but centrally appointed. Local leaders who had been active for many years without any formal administrative structure immediately challenged the authority of the new appointees. On the other hand, the relationship between these appointed leaders and official bodies like the consulate and the embassy was not clear. When US government officials and appointed tenth department representatives consulted or cooperated on projects, they managed to alienate both consular staff and local grassroots leaders.

Looking homeward

Some Haitians who achieved prosperity abroad had for many years turned back to Haiti and reinserted themselves into the society and politics of their former hometowns. As early as the 1960s Haitian transnational organizations dedicated themselves to the overthrow of Duvalier's regime. After unsuccessful attempts to lobby US officials to cut off aid to the regime, the groups continued to work together but shifted their attention from national politics to local issues. On one hand they assisted newly arrived immigrants to the United States, but in the final years of Baby Doc's regime they began to focus on the needs of their communities in Haiti. They initiated projects to supply the technology and resources needed to rebuild schools, install potable water fountains, or provide school supplies. These groups made their contributions rather discreetly until Duvalier's departure. Afterwards they formed a large, more widely publicized network of up to forty such organizations, known as the Fédération des Associations Régionales Haïtiennes à l'Etranger. Working in parallel with the more political tenth department, hometown associations looked back to Haiti to see how they might assist those they had left behind.

The activities of its members were impressive. For example, the Association des Fils et des Amis de Lavoute, founded in New York City in 1984, donated land for a marketplace, medical supplies, and football equipment. It also convinced the local board of education to support a school, helped to build a health clinic, and contributed to the rebuilding of a road. Similarly, the older Fraternité Valléenne, founded in 1977 in New York City, also built schools and health clinics and developed agricultural projects.

As the Haitian state grew less able to fulfill its obligations to provide social services, the organizations took on many projects. The New York City-based Organization for the Development of Lascahobas, founded in 1990, reshaped that town. In addition to building a new library, fully equipped with computers, opening a new sixty-bed hospital, and planning to increase the supply of electricity, it has assisted law enforcement, by putting up street signs and fencing in the town cemetery.

According to François Pierre-Louis, an expert on these organizations, the dynamics of these projects are striking. They demand collaboration between local residents and their Haitian donors abroad, and this can be a complicated affair. Those involved at the giving end maintain or increase their status and prestige within their hometown communities. They can exert influence by suggesting how people ought to vote, or by recommending friends and relatives for jobs. On the receiving end, some observers have argued, these interactions have led to the breakdown or softening of long-standing barriers between rural and urban inhabitants (though in this case there are also transnational boundaries, between rural Haitians and urban émigrés), thus empowering local residents by the subsequent changes in their communities. Others see a more ambivalent process, whereby the inequalities that allowed those to leave and prevented others from doing so are reproduced in the relationships between benefactor and beneficiary that emerge. The global dynamic that underlies the way these hometown associations work is one in which pressures to privatize and devolve power to the local level all too often reflect the abdication or inability of the state to provide social services. The lack of local resources makes it difficult to complete projects without outside assistance. Transnational relationships are built out of need, status and homesickness.[5]

Eventually, the pressure to assist Aristide from lobbying Haitians in alliance with US politicians became compelling enough for President Clinton to justify the use of force to reinstate him. In September 1994, a US-led military intervention returned Aristide to power. He served out the remainder of his term and oversaw the election of a successor. In the USA, Aristide's return felt like a bittersweet victory for some Haitian activists, who had to struggle with their ambivalence over the role of the USA and its military in Haitian politics. They responded with measured caution. Despite their hesitations, Aristide gave elite Haitians abroad an even more prominent place in his administration with the creation of the Ministry of Haitians Living Abroad. Its proposed activities included promotion of a positive image of Haiti in the media, a technical assistance program to send volunteering professionals to Haiti, a cultural program that promoted cultural events in both the United States and Haiti, a project directed at providing information to potential investors, and plans to support associations of Haitians abroad.

Ordinary Haitians responded more concretely, without the need for institutionalized structures. Residents in Miami in particular took advantage of the end of the embargo to reconnect with their friends and families in Haiti. For them, reopened borders meant a renewed flow of money, clothing, and food, which had been part of their role and responsibility as migrants to a wealthier country.

For many Haitian commercial establishments in Miami it became business as usual again, with its dependence on transnational ties. Agencies whose principal purpose was to wire money suddenly found their offices full of working-class Haitians eager to send money home. Radio stations whose advertisements had relied on crossing boundaries could resume their broadcasts, sponsored by travel agencies, realtors, shipping companies, and money exchange offices. Haitians crowded the docks, bringing goods to be shipped back to Haiti. These ranged from used clothing or car parts to new cars, thousands of tons of printing paper and building supplies. In material ways, and through a transnational informal economy, Haitian migrants relied on their position abroad to strengthen their ties to home.

Aristide's return and the vagaries of neoliberalism

But the reinstatement of Aristide brought demands for changes in economic policies, and eventually put many Haitians in a precarious condition. Even Marc Bazin, a Haitian economist who worked for the World Bank for eighteen years and a political opponent of Aristide's, observed that "the liberalization effort has taken place virtually without a decent level of external aid and Haiti has paid a very high price for its foray into globalization."[6] The Duvaliers had created what many observers have called a "predatory state." State-run companies, such as producers of cement and flour, were controlled by elites, as sources of personal enrichment. Corruption and little state control resulted in a bloated state sector that benefited elites but abandoned redistribution. To redress this situation the International Monetary Fund had called for a program of structural adjustment during the Duvalier regime and continued its demands when Aristide was elected. They concentrated especially on privatization of state-owned companies, envisioning their opening to foreign investors and efforts to increase the efficiency and transparency with which they delivered goods or services. Aristide navigated this situation by attempting to appease all sides, eventually alienating his supporters and doubters alike. During the campaign, his anti-capitalist rhetoric, appealing to a majority of Haitians, cast him as a radical to the bourgeoisie, American officials, and investors. His gestures towards the protection of private property, intended to allay the fears of the business class, fell on deaf ears. Yet, once elected, Aristide adopted many of the measures the IMF and World Bank had requested. His overthrow, the imposition of the embargo, and the many changes in government that ensued ensured that these would be implemented only piecemeal, if at all.

After his return the terms were tougher. Aristide and René Préval, who was elected in 1996, began to play cat and mouse with international finance institutions. Initially, Aristide accepted the Emergency Economic Recovery Program, drafted by a group that included representatives from the International Development Bank, the World Bank, the International Monetary Fund, and US Aid. This program contained many of the requirements from earlier structural adjustment programs, such as provisions for further openings of foreign investment opportunities, streamlining the public sector, and lifting price controls. It insisted particularly on the sale of many public enterprises. Smarck Michel, the prime minister, supported these measures, and enabled their implementation. Among the most significant measures was the privatization of the flour mill and cement plant.

But privatization came with a price. In the cement plant, for instance, only 150 of 667 employees kept their jobs. Vital service industries like Teleco, the telephone company, EDH, the electric company, as well as the ports and the airport, were privatized. One of the institutions immediately affected was the university, where low or negligible tuitions suddenly jumped tenfold. When students found out that arts fees would cost $1,088 rather than $30 per year, medical studies would rise to $900 from $50, or agronomy tuition would cost $1,599 instead of being free, they protested. These demonstrations effectively canceled a symposium intended to study the proposed university reform, and forced the resignation of the university's executive council. Aristide was forced to hold a meeting with fifty popular organizations at the national palace. An organization called the Collective for Mobilization against the IMF also protested the new policies. Aristide distanced himself from Smarck Michel and fired his finance minister, naming as his replacement someone much more critical of the imposed Emergency Economic Recovery Program, who suspended it. The task force in Washington responded in kind by suspending aid.

In the years following, aid was directly linked to perceived instability and fraud in political practices. The initial results, under Préval, were positive. Under the watchful eye of the managing director of the International Monetary Fund, sent to Haiti on the eve of the vote, parliament adopted the economic program and the IMF released $226 million in foreign aid. Once the bickering began between Aristide and Préval, however, it became much more difficult to hold on to this aid. When Aristide formed his own party, the Fanmi Lavalas, to challenge Préval's Organisation Politique Lavalas, he initiated a political crisis in which Préval refused to accept the results of the 1997 parliamentary elections. The IMF suspended aid until the holding of "free and fair" elections. Aristide won the 2000 election, and his party gained a majority in parliament. The coalition allied against him, known as the Democratic Convergence, declared the elections fraudulent. When the Organization of American States insisted on a recount and the Haitian CEP (Provisional Electoral Council) refused, the agencies again suspended aid, this time $600 million worth. Privatization continued throughout these crises. Without foreign aid, this proved disastrous to many Haitians.

Migration and desperation

Among many repercussions of this continuing privatization despite frequent suspension of foreign aid was the increased propensity of many Haitians to seek incomes abroad. Faced with a stagnating economy, diminishing agricultural productivity, and soaring unemployment, many Haitians saw emigration as their only option. The stories of those with some family connections and resources who could travel to the USA or Canada have been told with some frequency and great eloquence. Not so well accounted for are the journeys and lives of thousands of Haitians who remained within the Caribbean basin. While they also lead transnational lives deeply connected to the political and economic currents that dominate their country, their stories are much more dire.

Because of its proximity, the Turks and Caicos is a viable destination for some of the poorest Haitians. These six tiny islands near the Bahamas experienced a wave of emigration when salt mining, the principal source of income, declined in the 1960s. When the tourist industry started to pick up in the 1990s it created an increased demand for workers, particularly in construction. Haitians began to come to the Turks and Caicos to replenish a workforce long depleted by emigration. The Turks and Caicos' efforts to participate in the world tourist market facilitated the mobility of poor Haitians and perpetuated their marginal status in both places.

Anthropologist Dennis Brown has interviewed many of these people. Marie Antoine is forty-three years old and shares a small dwelling with four Haitian men, none of whom is her husband; he lives and works on the nearby island of Providenciales. Marie's house has no running water or electricity and the money she occasionally earns as a domestic servant allows her to buy water but not much else. Her inability to read has prevented her from finding steady work. She has left behind five children in Haiti, aged twenty-two, twenty, seventeen, fourteen, and eleven. Her mother takes care of them.

Some of the more recently arrived have not found permanent housing. Brown interviewed Jean Pierre, who had come from Haiti only five days earlier, having left a wife and children behind. Although he needed and wanted to find work, his prospects were not good, because he too was illiterate and lacked skills that would make him employable. Since he arrived illegally, he lived in bushes in a park, hiding from the authorities but exposing himself to hordes of mosquitoes and torrential rainstorms. Others have fled political persecution, such as François, who as a community leader became a target of the *Tonton Macoutes*. They killed his wife and made it clear that he would be killed as well if he did not leave. François needed to find work in order to support his children, whom he left in Haiti in the care of neighbors. There are some women living in the bushes as well. They are even more vulnerable than the men because they are raped or molested by locals who take advantage of their unwillingness to appeal to the police for protection.[7] These people have been driven away from Haiti by many of the same circumstances as those who ended up in the United States, Canada, or Europe. As the poorest emigrants, they have remained within the Caribbean and made it a receiving as well as a sending region in this stage of globalization.

Slightly more organized and systematized, and much greater in scope, is the migration of Haitians to the Dominican Republic, the other country on the island of Hispaniola. The Dominican Republic's economy is relatively strong: the GDP per capita is $830 for the Dominican Republic and $370 for Haiti, while yearly per capita growth rates are 2.3 per cent and .2 per cent respectively.

A globalizing trend in human rights practices has changed relationships between Haiti and the Dominican Republic. With the Duvaliers in power, Haitians were regularly conscripted as sugar workers in the Dominican Republic. After Baby Doc's departure human rights organizations such as Americas Watch and the National Coalition for Haitian Refugees were able to monitor these practices. This led to the expulsion of Haitians from the Dominican Republic in 1991, as these organizations argued for the termination of exploitative labor practices. But, ironically, the demand for labor and the need for work have continually propelled Haitians across the border. Some of them stay and others cross the border daily to find work and then go home at the end of the day. The intermingling of Haitians and Dominicans is so extensive that it seems impossible to count how many Haitians there are in the Dominican Republic. Estimates range from half a million to 1 million.

There is a large and busy traffic in Haitian children to the Dominican Republic to join the informal labor force there. These children supplement their family incomes or earn money for their own needs. Many work during the summer months and then return to school in the fall with clothing, shoes, and school supplies purchased with their wages. Others continue to work and quit school altogether.

A complex network of Haitians and Dominicans transports these children across the border. Most of this traffic takes place in the north. Assembled by Haitian "passeurs," these children are picked up by Dominican bus drivers who travel to various towns to fill their buses. They cross the border in either Ferrier or Capotille, where Dominican soldiers wave the busloads of children through. All these adult facilitators receive payment for their participation in this scheme. Some also manage to persuade a few children to act as mules and carry drugs back from the Dominican Republic to Haiti, thus profiting even more. There are also less exploitative ways for children to enter the Dominican Republic. On market days the border is completely open. Children can walk across with their families.

Children's labor is assigned according to age and gender. Those under five will work in urban areas, begging, usually with an older woman who poses as their mother. Between the ages of seven and twelve girls become domestic workers. Boys aged between five and twelve will shine shoes or beg, while boys twelve to seventeen work in construction, are street vendors, or do agricultural labor. The work varies, as does their treatment. Some can pay for a place to live (however inadequate) and a little food, or live close enough to churches and soup kitchens to benefit from their meal programs. Others find themselves more alone, and they often sleep in the streets, in cardboard boxes or in abandoned houses. Many are *restaveks* (literally "staying with," from the French "*reste avec*") which means that their families have sold them permanently and they will not return to Haiti. Often the girls are sexually exploited by the males of the families with which they live.

In some places the conditions are not so desperate. There are towns in the Dominican Republic where entire families have settled. In the best of circumstances they make up the informal labor force, most often selling goods in the streets or working in the fields. Occasionally, the children can attend school even though they work, and their families are integrated into social networks. These are the youngest transnational citizens. Although they do not vote and they are not likely to spend too much time or energy worrying about whether or how strongly they feel "Haitian," they do participate in and contribute to a transnational economy and society. This relationship, built on exploitation, nonetheless allows some Haitians to earn an income that might otherwise be unavailable to them.

Migration and conspiracy

Not all who enter the Dominican Republic are poor or powerless. The Dominican Republic has also been one of the centers of political organizing for Haitian exiles since the Duvalier days, when opposition parties gathered there and broadcast in Creole to Haiti. Joaquín Balaguer, president of the Dominican Republic, shut down these broadcasts in an effort to stifle the opposition to Duvalier. Recently, however, Balaguer and his successor, Leonel Fernández, have turned a blind eye to the Haitian operations of oppositional groups in their country. Both military and civilian groups working against Aristide have found support in the neighboring country in the past decade. In the last Aristide administration, which began in 2000 and ended with his departure in 2004, anti-Aristide military groups led by Guy Philippe waited just across the border. Philippe, a former police commander, had been involved in two failed coup attempts before leaving Haiti. He and Louis-Jodel Chamblain, convicted twice for his role in anti-Aristide death squads, gathered arms and men in the Dominican Republic before entering Haiti in late 2003 and instigating the crisis that led to Aristide's departure in February 2004.

While in the Dominican Republic, Philippe resided at least part of the time in the Hotel Santo Domingo, owned by a Cuban family, the Fanjuls, who left Cuba after the revolution and have become wealthy from their large sugar-cane business. This hotel was also the site of training sessions run by the International Republican Institute, a non-profit agency that describes itself as working to build democracy. This institute, closely allied to the Bush administration, held meetings in the Hotel Santo Domingo in 2002. They invited hundreds of members of groups opposed to Aristide to participate in what they called "political training." People from Aristide's own political party were not invited. Neither was Guy Philippe, who lived in the hotel at the time. But some observers have suggested that he received US support. The Bush appointee who led these meetings was Stanley Lucas, a member of the Haitian elite who frequently voiced his opposition to Aristide and his skepticism of political negotiations. Philippe asserts that he and Lucas have been friends for a long time. Lucas denies the connection. It may be futile to try to untangle these connections, but it is clear that these particular Haitians abroad wielded a great deal of power.

Influence, fragmentation, violence

As the state grew distracted with political crises and financially depleted, the Haitian diaspora's role became more acute. But even as some gained power and influence and participated more actively in elections, others, without the state's protection, became the targets of growing anti-Haitian sentiment. Aristide's second term as president was beset by conflicts over elections, and the unresolved political crisis contributed to his downfall. As the crisis deepened and the possibility that Aristide would again be forced to leave Haiti became likely, Haitians in the USA followed these developments with mixed feelings. In Miami, many expressed their continuing support for Aristide, their irritation with elites, and their fear of the rebels. To counter the strength of long-standing Aristide supporters such as Veye Yo, a group formed in 1978 to help those fleeing Duvalier, some Haitian Americans have banded together with emigrants of other Caribbean nations. The Haitian American Republican Caucus has allied itself with anti-Castro Cubans and anti-Chávez Venezuelans to strengthen their opposition to Aristide. Polls revealed these divisions among Haitians in the United States: 35 per cent of Haitian Americans polled in 2004 thought Aristide should resign; 57 per cent thought he should remain because he had been elected by a majority of Haitians in 2000; 13 per cent said they did not know.

The leading candidates in the 2005/06 elections went out of their way to acknowledge the tenth department. Aware that 80 per cent of college-educated Haitians live overseas, and assuming that the entire Haitian middle class has left Haiti, eight candidates campaigned in Boston, New York, and Miami. Others went to France. For the first time in history, presidential debates in a Haitian election were held outside Haiti, in Boston. Marc Bazin, one of the candidates, conducted meetings in Brooklyn at which he reminded audiences that he had lived in the United States for eighteen years and was thus uniquely qualified to attend to their needs. Regardless of their position on Aristide, all the candidates campaigning in the USA promised to implement dual citizenship. Aristide had in fact supported a constitutional amendment that would have allowed dual citizenship, but parliament was dissolved before the amendment was made law.

Dual citizenship would have broadened the pool not only of voters but of candidates as well. Among those blocked by the citizenship requirements was the popular Dumarsais Siméus, a multi-billionaire born in Haiti but residing in Texas for forty-five years. Despite this enforcement of the electoral rules about dual citizenship, many politicians are in fact residents of two worlds. Interim prime minister Gerard Latortue, a resident of Boca Raton, Florida, was living there when he was selected for the post, and planned to return there after his tenure. Jean Claude Desgranges, a supporter of Bazin who divides his time between Haiti and Florida, flaunted his de facto dual citizenship during a campaign rally in Brooklyn, when he declared, in Creole, "I'm of the tenth department just like you. I'm a true Haitian, just like you. You are all living as Haitians and you are all going to die as Haitians."

President elect René Préval traveled to the United States and Canada soon after his victory in the elections of early 2006, demonstrating his understanding of the importance of the tenth department. He met with groups of Haitians in both New York and Washington. In New York, he attended to various constituencies. Those who could afford it paid $100 a plate for a benefit reception at a hotel near the United Nations. In a less formal setting, on the Queens campus of City University of New York, Préval addressed nearly two thousand supporters. This was reported as an ebullient gathering, with Préval at his charming best surrounded by the leaders of the New York branch of the Fanmi Lavalas.

At the same time, Haitians in the Dominican Republic fell victim to suspicion and violence. In August 2005, the body of a thirteen-year-old Dominican boy was discovered in Pueblo Nuevo, a town in the northwestern province of Valverde in the Dominican Republic.

Residents suspected an undocumented Haitian migrant named Federico Pierre, and embarked on a violent retaliatory spree. They set fire to the homes of Haitians and attacked them with machetes, rocks, and clubs. In a few hours they managed to burn down three houses and injure dozens of Haitians. The Dominican police and military detained and deported hundreds of Haitian agricultural and construction workers. This incident sparked many similar ones, resulting in the deaths of dozens of Haitians and the deportation of thousands more. That same month, three Haitian migrants in the town of Haina, near the capital city of Santo Domingo, were bound, gagged, and set on fire. All three died within a week of the attacks. In December, an episode in which a Dominican money changer tried to collect on a debt from a Haitian worker set off a series of violent acts, starting with the money changer's murder. After police reported that they had arrested seven Haitian suspects, Dominican residents set fire to thirty-five houses in which Haitians lived. In the days that followed some ten Haitians ended up dead, and many more wounded. Hundreds of Haitians either returned to Haiti of their own volition or were sent back after police roundups. Dominican coffee growers, who depended on Haitian labor, worried about the harvest.

Haitians do not stand by helplessly when such violent incidents occur. Some have formed advocacy groups to assist Haitians in the Dominican Republic with legal and social problems. The Movimiento de Mujeres de Dominico-Haitianas Inc. (MUDHA), founded by Sonia Pierre, is one of these groups. Pierre, a Dominican-Haitian herself, created this organization in the early 1980s to protect the rights of Dominicans of Haitian descent, who even if second- or third-generation Dominicans are routinely denied citizenship. Her organization provides basic services for women and children, including schools and adult education centers, health clinics, and daycare facilities. In addition, she has begun to work to ensure that Dominicans of Haitian descent enjoy the citizenship rights (which for children include schooling) that were legally granted to little effect. Human rights organizations have begun to recognize her work. In 2003 she was awarded Amnesty International's Ginetta Sagan Award, and in 2006 she received the RFK Memorial Human

Rights Award. Other groups have begun to work with recent migrants as well as Dominicans of Haitian descent. The National Coalition for Haitian Rights (NCHR), founded in 1982 and originally dedicated to protect the rights of Haitians in the United States, in 1999 began working to prevent the expulsions of Haitians from the Dominican Republic and to assist Haitians to obtain residency or citizenship papers.

Conclusion

The practice of transnational citizenship has expanded, as revealed in the example of Haitians in the USA assisting Haitians who are not in Haiti anymore to achieve legal status in the Dominican Republic. These groups and the people they work with bypass state institutions even as they rely on the state for legal support and legitimization. They understand citizenship in different combinations of official and affective structures. They are changing the definitions and practices of citizenship, and of nation. This story has no ending, but this chapter ends by emphasizing the diversity of experiences of those Haitians who leave Haiti, as well as of those who remain but whose lives are touched in some way by the movement of people and goods. Although Haitians have been moving for many years, they have recently devised new ways to be transnational citizens, for better or for worse.

2 | Sell it to save it

The stories tell of increasing hunger and desperation, a desperation that drove thousands of Cubans to build flimsy rafts by tying a few inner tubes together and then launch them from downtown Havana itself, jumping off the Malecón and heading out across the short but notoriously dangerous 90-mile passage to Florida. These were the stories of the summer of 1994, at the beginning of the Orwellian "Special Period in the Time of Peace," as the effects of the collapse of the Eastern bloc and dwindling Soviet subsidies forced Cubans to resort to desperate measures. Though Havanans often complain, they seldom riot. Yet they did during that summer; and soon after, the government, which had been acting behind the scenes to alleviate serious fuel and food shortages, took measures that would affect the daily lives of its citizens. When people talk about that period, they divide it into "before the riots" and "after the riots." They talk about the way that Castro himself walked downtown, into the middle of the rioters, and silenced them with his presence. They talk about changes afterwards, and how things got better, even though the Soviet Union's subsidies, which had reached $6–8 billion annually, were gone forever and the enduring US economic embargo was soon reinforced and extended by the Helms-Burton Act. Pizza stands sprang up in the streets of Havana. Dollar stores, where, as the name implies, US currency was the medium of exchange, began to stock a wider variety of imported crackers, juice, and candy. Farmers' markets now displayed and sold more than just a few token piles of wilted greens.

When academics write about that period, they note the economic recovery since then, and examine Cuba's complex relationship with market forces and globalization, and its own unwavering commitment to socialism. They tend to ignore their dramatic earlier predictions at the beginning of the Special Period that Castro's regime, if it remained stubbornly revolutionary, would not last. But scholarly voices have been effectively drowned out by the burgeoning industry of Cuban memoirists for whom Cuba's survival in the Special Period has proved a fruitful subject. Thus, Cubans who have left for America, Americans who have traveled in Cuba, Europeans who brought their Cuban wives back home, novelists who write about Cuban women who marry Europeans, former diplomats, combatants in Angola or the Bay of Pigs, Castro's relatives, and Che's relatives, have filled bookstore shelves with their accounts. The question of "what happens in the transition?" so irritating to Cubans (who are living what can only be imagined as a transition) and so fascinating to visitors becomes more and more irrelevant, just like the embargo that has failed after nearly five decades to bring the communist regime down. Cuba has found ways to "sell" its revolution, in order to keep it alive.

This chapter will concentrate on the ways in which even the Caribbean economy most "closed" in theory has taken advantage of the new and more concentrated flows of capital that characterize contemporary globalization. When one source of foreign capital disappeared, others replaced it, allowing Cuba to recover from an economic crisis that might have turned into a political crisis. The chapter looks at the ways in which Cuba has reinserted itself into global markets, beginning shortly before the fall of the Soviet Union, and accelerating ever since. The Cuban government has concentrated on three main areas of growth: tourism, biotechnology, and mining. In tourism, it has fallen in step with many other parts of the Caribbean, seeking to expand that industry but also finding ways to capitalize on its unique status as a socialist state. The biotech industry has sprung from the government's commitment to healthcare and education, taking advantage of its early investments and well-trained doctors, especially in relation to the rest of Latin America. And in mining, since there was less activity during the years of a closer relationship to the Soviet Union, there has been room for explosive growth.

Coinciding with these changes in Cuba has been a sea change in Latin American politics, which have leaned to the left especially in the last ten years or so. While Cuba has been adapting to a market economy, Latin American nations such as Venezuela and Bolivia have made strong statements critiquing the history of their own engagements not just with market economies but with neoliberal hegemonies. This has strengthened ideological links between Cuba and Latin America, as well as reinforcing Cuba's long-standing dual identity as both a Caribbean and a Latin American nation.

The chapter ends with observations regarding Cuba's increasingly complicated relationship with the United States and with Cuban emigrants who reside there. The embargo, which has remained unexamined by the US government for many years, has recently been both more vehemently defended and more widely criticized by different sectors of Americans as well as Cuban exiles, most of whom have ended up in the United States. Although the latter have been more visible in some ways than their Haitian counterparts, in the end they have shaped domestic Cuban politics mostly by strengthening Cuban resolve to resist their hostility. At the same time, new generations of Cuban-Americans have adopted more conciliatory perspectives and in some cases have worked to reconcile the two countries. The USA and Cubans abroad seem increasingly fragmented with regard to Cuba, while Cuba itself implements measures that ensure its survival, if not as a purely socialist economy, as a fascinating hybrid of socialism, capitalism, pragmatism, and tenacity.

Negotiating socialism

Unlike Haiti, which, despite its many regime changes over the last twenty years, saw little change in its economic situation, subject as it was to powerful external constraints, Cuba has experienced a number of shifts in economic policy in decades of one-man rule. The declaration of a Marxist-Leninist program in 1961 nationalized the economy and created priorities in health and education that have remained defining elements for the regime. But the path to these ends has not always been straight. Cuba has shown remarkable flexibility in its policy shifts, meeting challenges with adept responses that have enabled the revolution to survive the end of the cold war.

Following an early transitional period of uncertainty and experimentation between 1959 and 1961, the revolution settled down to

pursue its idealistic socialist goals. Political structures were central-
ized and the economy was nationalized. After flirting briefly with
reducing the importance of sugar to the economy, Castro realized
that sugar was still the largest potential source of revenue. In this
phase, Castro rode the wave of youthful enthusiasm and demanded
sacrifice and austerity from Cubans. To participate fully in the revolution, they were asked to contribute to collective goals, shun material
rewards, and behave according to Che Guevara's idea of the "New
Man" as disciplined, principled, ascetic citizens. The battle over
consumerism began in this period, as a rationing system was set
up to ensure an equitable distribution of goods. This worked, to a
certain extent, but it also gave rise to a lively black market.

The disastrous sugar campaign of 1970 marked a shift in government policies. In need of revenue for his increasingly expensive social
experiment, Castro had called for a harvest of 10 million tons, which
would have been the largest harvest in Cuban history. Public relations campaigns exhorted Cubans to pitch in and work on weekends.
When the final tally amounted to only 8.5 million tons, the revolution
teetered on the edge of legitimacy. In a brilliant move, Castro offered
to resign, assuring the crowds gathered at the Plaza of the Revolution
that he was unworthy of their respect. Cubans still remember that
they refused to allow him to resign, swore their loyalty to him, and
promised to carry on. In spite of the seeming tenacity of the Cuban
populace, this moment of crisis also witnessed significant changes
in policy. The ensuing "retreat to socialism" included limited market
openings, some democratic reforms encouraging participation at the
local level, and the implementation of a series of material incentives
as a reward for productive work. Lasting until 1986, this period saw
modest economic recovery, the opening of new political spaces, and
the initiation of trade with Latin America and Europe.

In 1986, however, criticism of these transformations worked
its way into government policy, which returned to the rhetorical
exhortations of the earlier years. Dubbed the period of "rectifica-
tion of errors and negative tendencies," the late 1980s appeared
to be a time of reassertion of ideological purity. Market reforms
and material incentives disappeared, while images of Che Guevara
and reminders of the virtues of voluntary and collective labor re-

appeared. Behind the scenes, however, Castro seemed to realize that some kind of engagement with global markets was going to prove necessary for the survival of the regime. Even as the same business enterprises that had been tacitly (or not so tacitly) encouraged in the 1970s were being accused of betraying socialist ideals with their capitalist endeavors, the government moved toward market-oriented reforms. It began to allow enterprises of mixed private and public ownership of the means of production, to open up to international markets and market prices, and to decentralize decision-making. But it also increased surveillance of dissidents, made it more difficult for Cubans to travel out of the country, and imposed burdensome taxes on family-run restaurants (*paladares*) and rooming houses. This tricky combination of pragmatic economic policies and steadfastly anti-capitalist and anti-imperialist rhetoric would become one of the main features of the post-1989 Cuban economy and society.[1]

Castro would publicly emphasize his commitment to his revolution at every opportunity, including during a visit by Gorbachev on the eve of what would turn out to be momentous change for everyone involved. If anything, the reforms already occurring in the Soviet Union served as a foil for Cuba's persistent ideological purity. When Gorbachev came to Cuba in April 1989, American commentators compared and contrasted the Soviet leader's conciliatory gestures toward the United States with the intransigent Fidel Castro's forceful anti-US rhetoric and determination to stay the communist course. In a repeat of previous cold war scripts, the visit to Cuba became linked to regional issues. More pressing than the fate of Cuba, whose influence was seen as waning, were issues surrounding the revolutionary government in Nicaragua, the Contra rebels supported by the United States, and the insurgents in El Salvador fighting to overthrow a rightist regime. Both the United States and the Soviet Union used the opportunity of the visit to conduct a dialogue, from which Cuba was largely absent, about the fate of these struggles.

Beyond the attempts to manipulate Central American conflicts, Gorbachev's visit was an elaborately staged performance by both heads of state. Although journalists' descriptions of the Cuba Gorbachev encountered focused on drab, faltering aspects of revolutionary life and the weakness and dependence of the economy, by the end of the visit it was Gorbachev who was perceived as "wilting" and Castro as "towering." Cubans and Soviets watched the dance with fascination: despite rumors of incompatibility or even hostility, the two leaders hugged, waved at crowds of Cubans as they drove past in their motorcade, walked arm in arm, and protected one another from reporters' questions. As the visit wore on, signs of tensions began to emerge: while Gorbachev tried to mollify the United States, Castro delivered a blistering attack (as Gorbachev "listened with a grim expression"). Although they signed a treaty "condemning the use of force as an instrument of foreign policy," Gorbachev vocally criticized the export of revolution while Castro asserted that "like Che Guevara, I am against the use of capitalist mechanisms to build socialism."[2]

Castro emerged as more determined than ever to pursue his revolution. Only a few observers wondered how much of this was a performance. Had the two leaders agreed, behind the scenes, that reformist measures would prove unavoidable? Had Castro blustered in public and conceded in private? Perhaps these observers were aware of the changes Castro had already initiated, suspecting maybe that Soviet support would not last for ever. Two years later the economic crisis that resulted from the elimination of Soviet subsidies would force him to make all kinds of concessions, envisioned or not.

Castro has not engineered Cuba's transformation by working alone. According to Jon Lee Anderson, several members of his government have been key players in this complex moment. Along with Raúl Castro, who heads the military and serves as defense minister, three men have emerged as the architects (with Castro's guidance and blessing) of the new Cuba. They are Ricardo Alarcón, president of Cuba's National Assembly, Felipe Pérez Roque, the foreign minister, and Vice-President Carlos Lage, who is said to have controlled many of the recent changes in economic policy. These three play quite different roles from one another, and herein may be the source of Cuba's seemingly contradictory course. When Carlos Lage formulated the plans to open the economy and oversaw their implementation, he set off a series of chain reactions. The successful efforts to generate income for the revolutionary government created a social class of consumers, an important and visible contrast to previous years. Many Cubans were increasingly less self-conscious about appearing to have more possessions than their neighbors. This in turn animated an ideological counter-campaign to remind Cubans that the revolution was not over even as it was making some concessions to a market economy.

Ricardo Alarcón and Pérez Roque served as the public face of these ideological battles. Alarcón was appointed leader of the National Assembly in 1993, after long experience abroad as Cuba's ambassador to the United Nations from 1966 until 1992. The years in New York led some Americans to view him as a moderate, but he has in fact been the driving force behind two vociferously anti-US campaigns: the Elián González case, and the trials of the Cuban Five. When the six-year-old Elián González was rescued aboard a raft off the coast of Florida on Thanksgiving Day in 1999, a battle ensued over whether he ought to be sent back to Cuba, where his father resided, or remain in Miami with relatives who had left Cuba long before. Both the Cuban exile community and the Cuban government used the case to rally loyalties and demonize their opponent. In Havana, countless rallies featured Cubans waving flags and demanding the return of Elián. When he did finally return, Cuba was said to have triumphed over not just the United States, but also those exiled Cubans who opposed Castro's regime so tenaciously. The campaigns surrounding the Cuban Five involve Cuba's demand that five men arrested in the United States for having served as spies for Cuba be returned to Cuba and avoid trial. The public campaign involved ubiquitous pamphlets, billboards, and television ads, urging the release of the "Five Heroes." Pérez Roque has also contributed to the project of ideological renewal as head of the recently created Battle of Ideas, which intended to resuscitate flagging enthusiasm and moral purity with programs such as the School for Social Workers. The school targeted underprivileged young people and trained them as social workers, who would in turn battle corruption through various methods. Whether these are working is hard to tell. But they do lend the revolution a contradictory tone, as battles for moral purity and loyalty to the revolutionary cause sit alongside the very visible changes wrought by economic openings. In some ways, however, these trends are not so contradictory. Much of the ideological work in recent years has been explicitly anti-USA, rather than anti-capitalist. This is in keeping with the nationalist fervor that guided the earliest years of the revolution, before it declared itself to be Marxist-Leninist. In this instance, globalization, which is often said to eliminate or diminish the significance of national boundaries, has fortified official Cuban nationalism.[3]

Tourism

Dramatic statistics describe Cuba's successful re-engagement with the tourist industry. Foreign visitors to the island totaled 370,000 in 1990. Ten years later, in 2000, that total had jumped to 1.8 million. By 2000, tourism had become the largest single source of income, rising from 4 per cent in 1990 to 43 per cent in 2000. In terms of employment, estimates indicate that between 100,000 and 150,000 Cubans are directly dependent on tourism, while another 200,000 in related sectors produce goods and services for the tourist industry.

Glossy brochures have assisted this transformation. Most of them sell sun and sand, with idiosyncratic bits thrown in to help travelers differentiate between Cuba and other Caribbean playgrounds. They promise day-long excursions on horseback, hikes along the beach, and opportunities to snorkel or ride jet-skis. Lunchtime meals seem traditionally Cuban: they eat pork roast, rice, beans, and vegetable and fruit, accompanied by Cuban beer or Tropicola. Yet of this "typical Cuban fare," all but the rice and beans are out of reach for many Cubans, for whom vegetables, fruit, and especially meat remain an occasional luxury. Some brochures also advertise rides in venerable old cars or trips to Hemingway's marina. A visitor encounters "classic Cuba" from the perspective of the 1950s, when relations between Cuba and the United States were, in the words of an eminent historian, characterized by "ties of singular intimacy."[4] Daily ferries shipped passengers and new Chevrolets, Fords, Studebakers and Packards from Miami to Havana. Writers like Hemingway could travel to Cuba for the weekend to fish, eat, and drink; the traces they left behind have become main attractions for curious visitors, whether aware of or oblivious to the ironies in which they participate. The brochures make no mention of these ironies.

When tourist guidebooks deliberately sell history, that history is colonial. Descriptions of Trinidad, a town built with sugar money in southern Cuba, or even of recently refurbished La Habana Vieja, where most of the original buildings stand, emphasize the sixteenth and seventeenth centuries and the connections to Spain, or, in the case of Cienfuegos, France. Perfectly restored churches and convents allude to a period Cubans since then have both embraced and struggled against: the wars of independence and the language of anti-colonialism jostling against the proud claims of many Cubans to Spanish blood, and, more concretely, to European Union passports.

It would be easy for a visitor to overlook the history of the country since 1959. The landmarks and artefacts of the revolution itself, as a historical process, are not necessarily presented as part of a vacation package. A great deal of the tourism that has developed depends on all-inclusive stays at resorts, many of which are far from urban centers. When visitors do want to see the city, the government seems to prefer that they take guided tours, experiencing it mostly from air-conditioned buses with well-trained guides. Visitors to Havana on guided tours will drive past the plazas and buildings instantly recognizable from photographs of Castro's speeches, but they will only get to see the inside of the Museum of the Revolution if they choose to stay two days rather than one. Visitors to the Bay of Pigs will learn about a turning point in the early revolution, but they will not be overly taxed with information: "finally, a place where recent history was made – the Bay of Pigs. Your English speaking guide will explain its history and significance to the Cuban people. There may not be so much excitement at the site now, but in 1961 when the CIA trained and financed an attempted invasion, which was successfully defeated by locals, it made a great impact on the future of Cuba." It is preferable, it seems, for visitors to distract themselves with the natural beauty than to dwell on the historical significance of the Bay of Pigs: "This bay is also quite picturesque, so afterwards why not have a dip in the Caribbean sea!"

But tourists probably do not spend much time reading guidebooks or visiting industrial parks. What they see on the streets of Havana and other towns are patient people in long lines, young women in skimpy clothing, and the often mentioned "dollar stores" where they can duck in and buy cold water or crackers, or if the store is attached to a hotel, wine or chocolate. They see the signs of the growing tourist sector as they walk past handsome new hotels or zip around idling tour buses in their cocotaxis, the new sunny yellow scooters that charge twice as much as regular taxis.

In the early days, their hotel choice was limited and the government carefully tracked their movements. They shook their heads at spending a dollar for water and the equivalent of a penny for coffee, but they learned to keep their water bottles to give them to children clamoring for them in the street. They stayed in hotels that barred Cubans from entering, or in Varadero, a whole town that tried to keep Cubans, except for hotel workers, out. The influx of visitors has opened contacts. Cubans come and go in hotels, to send emails or faxes or to have a beer at the bar. Some Cubans persist in renting rooms to foreigners in their homes despite exorbitant taxes and arbitrary changes of the rules.

Early visitors also had to learn to handle many different currencies. Cuban pesos were not really necessary, but once you began to use them a whole world of goods obtainable only in Cuban pesos opened up. With Cuban pesos you could go to the Cuban bookstores, stand in line for street pizza or buy sweets and coffee to stave off hunger pangs. Convertible pesos were supposed to be the equivalent of US dollars and were used for salaries of Cubans working for joint ventures. But otherwise it was not clear why a visitor would want to use them, since dollars would do. US dollars were illegal until 1993. After that, everyone wanted them, except those Cubans who saw them as signs of imperialism. Using dollars was prohibited again in 2004. Visitors and Cubans who received dollars as remittances were required to change them and use convertible pesos. The government takes 20 per cent from each exchange of dollars into convertible pesos. It has devised a way to keep dollars for itself.

Many have noticed and written about the rise of prostitution in connection to the growing tourist sector, and of the porous boundaries between prostitution, friendship, affection, and love. These stories range from Cuban medical students who meet foreign men and then get taken dancing or for dinner, to fourteen-year-old girls whose families desperately need the money they earn from sex work, to the scores of Cuban women who marry Europeans and move to Italy or Spain, some happily, others cynically, others tragically.

Inevitably, visitors encounter the question of race, as the tourist industry has changed racial dynamics in multiracial Cuba. On one hand, easy access to dollars via employment in the tourist industry (mostly in tips) and the flow of remittances have skewed incomes, lifting those of non-blacks, for they are the preferred employees as well as the major recipients of money from abroad. Most Cubans who left Cuba, especially the earlier waves, thought of themselves as white. When they send money, it is to their families, most of whom also think of themselves as white. On the other hand, many Cubans who participate in the informal economy would describe themselves as black or mulatto. This does less to balance the distribution of dollars or other income discrepancies than to label people by making their cash source visible. Those who have dollars to convert can buy appliances and nicer toys for their children, as much milk, fruit juice, and cooking oil as they are willing to pay for, and makeup, nail polish, or blue jeans.

In La Habana Vieja, the heart of revived urban tourism, cafés line the shady Plaza de Armas, and artisans sell their crafts just like anywhere else. Many of the most beautifully restored hotels are in this neighborhood, including the famous Ambos Mundos, where Hemingway is said to have stayed. Nestled among the restored museums, new galleries, and lovely churches, a Benetton store proclaims Cuba's engagement with global capitalism. But, unlike many other places in the Caribbean, the neighborhood of La Habana Vieja benefits from tourism in an unusual way. Since the renovation is controlled by the state, and in particular by the Oficina del Historiador de la Ciudad (Office of the Historian of the City), a portion of the revenues from these tourist enterprises is used for social services like daycare centers and health clinics for Cubans residing in the neighborhood. The money goes only so far, however, as evidenced by the stark contrast between the perfect cobblestones in the plaza and the potholed streets and crumbling buildings a few blocks away.

Cuba attracts far more than just the sun and sand crowd. University students can study Spanish at the University of Havana.

Church groups often travel on missions, to deliver goods and get to know Cuba's growing congregations. Those concerned with the environment can find ecotourist packages or work on an organic farm for a few days. Dancers and musicians can attend workshops on Afro-Cuban music and dance. For all these groups, the attraction seems more Cuba itself as one of the few remaining socialist states. Realizing this, the Cuban government has found ways to benefit financially, as most of these experiences come with a large price tag.

Mining

While Che T-shirts and the Buena Vista Social Club may be the most visible markers of Cuba's entrance into the global economy, they are hardly the only ones. Far less visible but no less important, the burgeoning mining industry has been a growth area since 1986. A number of factors have contributed to making mining, particularly in nickel, highly lucrative. In 1989, Sherritt, a Canada-based refining company, began to seek new sources of unrefined nickel for its smelters in Alberta, which were running at 40 per cent capacity. Before then, they had obtained ore from the Soviet Union, which had received it from Cuba in exchange for oil. With the defunct Soviet Union no longer the middleman, Sherritt looked directly to Cuba as a source of ore. Although it had found some Canadian sources at Timmins Lake and Nameau Lake, they could not compete with what was available from Cuba. In 1990, Sherritt obtained 6,000 tons of ore from Cuban mines, the beginning of a rapidly expanding relationship.

At first, Sherritt kept this source secret. By 1993, however, enough oblique references in the press confirmed US suspicions that Cuba was the principal supplier. The United States responded by refusing to purchase any more nickel from Sherritt. Although it amounted to 30 per cent of Sherritt's client base, the mining company did not end its relationship with Cuba. Instead, it formed a joint venture with the Cuban government. It was the largest of its kind at the time, and the most significant Canadian participation in the Cuban economy. Raw ore would be extracted from the mine in Moa, Cuba, and transported to Fort Saskatchewan, for processing. In accordance with Cuban law, Sherritt owned 49 per cent of the enterprise, while the Cuban government had a 51 per cent share. Sherritt invested close to $150 million to upgrade and expand the Cuban mine. In five years production doubled, from 13,000 tons to 24,000 tons annually. Sherritt has been one of the main reasons for the rapid growth of Canadian trade with Cuba, which grew from $216 million in 1990 to $595 million in 1995, and reached $917 million in 2004.

The United States government was not happy about this new relationship, and it has on occasion attempted to intervene. Invoking the Helms-Burton Act of 1996, which aims to discourage foreign companies from doing business with Cuba, it has prevented Sherritt executives from entering the United States. More important, the United States has filed a lawsuit against Sherritt, arguing that the joint venture is using property that was expropriated from US citizens without compensation at the onset of the 1959 revolution. Sherritt responded by creating a second company to deal only with Cuban operations. Nickel has proved lucrative enough to enable Sherritt to withstand attempts to interfere with its business. But the conflict continues. In 2006, the Commission for Assistance for a Free Cuba, a study group created by President Bush, recommended among other things a crackdown on nickel exports, which it claimed made up half of Cuba's foreign income. Nickel prices are higher than ever, and the company hopes to increase its production by 50 per cent in the next few years. The commission clearly wished to squeeze the Castro regime by invoking the Helms-Burton Act. But this will be hard to do. The nickel is sold mostly to Europe for the production of stainless steel and is hence nearly impossible to trace as it becomes part of a host of manufactured goods from jet engines to trendy refrigerators. In addition, Sherritt has diversified, making it even more difficult to control. It is now also involved in cobalt production, and oil, gas, and soybean operations.[5]

Biotech

Even before the influx of tourists and the renewed success in mining, the Cuban government was seeking ways to generate revenue. It was in 1986, with seeming prescience, that the Cuban government made a large-scale investment in the biotechnology industry. That year it established the Center for Genetic Engineering and Biotechnology (CIGB), an ultra-modern research facility on the outskirts of Havana. By 1998, it housed 700 researchers and has remained a priority through the most difficult moments of post-Soviet hardship: even in 1990 Castro was able to invest over $1 billion in the center. Many observers have noted the importance of scientific achievements in the continuing self-justifications of socialist Cuba. When the economic crisis hit, much of the research energy was directed towards practical findings in agriculture, forestry, and marine biology. Scientists cloned new seeds and developed fertilizers that did not require imported materials. Yet this research also had markets abroad in mind. The plan envisioned the biotech and medical industries serving the revolution in three different ways: the introduction of vaccines and medicines that could be marketed overseas, the export of medical personnel to poor countries all over the world, and the development of some of the most impressive treatment facilities in Latin America to give foreigners a "dose" of Cuban medicine.

Cubans have succeeded in devising several medical products for marketing abroad. They were the first to develop a meningitis B vaccine, and by 1998 were also producing monoclonal antibodies and streptokinase to break up blood clots. They worked on less expensive versions of many medical products, such as testing kits for AIDS, neural tube defects, hepatitis and syphilis as well as vaccines against hepatitis C, dengue and cholera. The Center of Molecular Immunology has focused on various cancer remedies. All these products were meant to appeal to neighboring Latin American and Caribbean nations who were too poor to afford the kinds of prices charged by Cuba's competitors, including US-based pharmaceuticals. Once it began to pay more attention to its sales and marketing, the Cuban biotech industry proved quite successful. In 1998, it brought in $100 million.

In recent years the marketing branch of CIGB has participated in a number of joint ventures that have taken Cuba's biotech industry well beyond nearby Latin America and the Caribbean to many Asian countries. In 2004 it claimed it was marketing its products in at least fifty countries. For example, Heber Biotech, the marketing and sales branch of the CIGB, reported in 2002 that it had just signed a joint venture agreement with Bioven Holdings of Malaysia. The agreement had three phases: the first would concentrate on marketing and distribution of Heber's biotech products in Cuba, Malaysia and other Asian countries. A second phase would focus more on developing joint research projects by the two countries. In the final phase, Heber Biotech would set up plants locally, in Malaysia.

Cuba is building biotech connections with many other countries. In Sri Lanka, where many Cuban doctors assisted in 2004's tsunami relief effort, the two governments have agreed to exchange specialists and research findings. Sri Lanka will undoubtedly benefit from Cuba's work on diseases like malaria and dengue fever. In 2002, doctors from Mozambique took part in a special course at the Cuban Center for Genetic Engineering and Biotechnology. In 2006, Cuba agreed to send Vietnam vaccines to help immunize the Vietnamese against hepatitis B and hemophilus influenza type B, which causes a type of meningitis. Also in 2006, India and Cuba created a company called Biocon Biopharmaceutical to manufacture and market vaccines. The reach of Cuban biotech extends even to the United States. In December 2004 the CIGB announced that it would begin testing its lung cancer vaccine in the United States. An agreement with CancerVax, a California-based biotech company, should facilitate the transfer of knowledge and technology from Cuba to the USA.

One strategy that has created both political and economic capital for the revolutionary regime almost since its inception has been the export of Cuban doctors and healthcare. The first medical brigade, comprising fifty-six doctors, was sent to Algeria in 1963. Since then, doctors and healthcare workers from Cuba have worked in numerous poor nations. In the 1970s and 1980s, sixty countries in Latin America, Africa, Asia, and the Middle East received medical assistance that included not just personnel, but supplies, medications, and the construction of healthcare facilities. Many of these healthcare workers ended up in rural or isolated areas and worked for up to two years before being sent home. Cuban officials claim that between 1965 and 1990, half a million Cubans provided healthcare services overseas. Even more dramatic are the ratios of aid workers to inhabitants, especially when compared to the United States. While in January 1990 Cuba boasted one civilian aid worker for every 228 inhabitants, the USA could muster only one civilian aid worker for every 35,670 inhabitants. This practice legitimized the revolutionary state in the eyes of foreigners and demonstrated to Cubans their status as an aid-giving nation. In addition, if less noteworthy, it brought in revenue, as some of the recipient countries paid for the medical brigades.[6]

Despite, or perhaps because of, its success, the project has met with criticism, both at home and abroad. Domestically, Cubans are afraid that the export of so many doctors will drain the country of these skilled resources and thus make access to healthcare more difficult. They also point to the bitter irony of foreigners receiving medicines manufactured in Cuba, which they themselves cannot obtain. Abroad, resident medical practitioners often protest that they are being replaced by Cubans.

While Cubans may bemoan the lack of easy availability of items like aspirin or vitamins, statistically their health has improved since the onset of the Special Period. Infant mortality rates decreased from 1994 to 2000, as did other indicators, such as death from cardiovascular diseases. As the government generated revenues from various sources, it devoted some of these funds to the healthcare system. While healthcare expenditures were 7.5 per cent of the national budget in 1994, they rose to 11 per cent in 2000. This has enabled the Cuban government to increase the numbers of healthcare workers at home even as it sends others abroad, and to continue to fund primary healthcare and public health programs.[7]

Cubans at home also receive regular reports about their compatriots abroad, as the health delivery project involves an intense publicity campaign. Television and radio reporters accompany the brigades and regularly chronicle their activities. As Castro explained in a 1999 speech, the government had invested in television cameras and recorders and paid the travel expenses of numerous journalists so that they might visit the medical brigades and report back on their progress. With a rather sentimental eye he envisioned "families who will not only be able to hear the voices of their loved ones, but also see the images of their mothers, or sisters, or husbands on television."[8]

The other aspect of this project involves educating potential doctors from all over Latin America and the Caribbean. At the Escuela

Latinoamericana, hundreds of students receive instruction each year. The Caribbean School opened in Santiago with the specific aim of reaching out to Haitian students, who also needed language training, since the language of instruction is Spanish. In a much publicized maneuver, Castro offered scholarships to students from Harlem in New York City, reminding the world again of his commitment to the health and welfare not just of Cubans, but of disadvantaged groups everywhere, even in the United States.

More tourism

In some ways the cleverest tactic, however, has been the promotion of "health tourism." This comes in many guises, ranging from hospitals for cancer and AIDS treatments, to plastic surgery and detox clinics, to spas that feature mineral baths and programs to counteract the stress and demands of the capitalist world. The idea of linking health resorts with nearby hospitals began with Servimed, a state-run company that in the late 1980s realized the advantages of selling healthcare as part of a vacation in Cuba. As early as 1995 Cuba reported earnings of $23 million for treatment of foreigners for vitilgio, psoriasis, retinosis, HIV care, cosmetic surgery, and much else. The following year up to seven thousand foreigners visited Cuba for healthcare. Although the numbers fluctuate, thousands continue to arrive. Some come because the kinds of treatments offered are not available in their countries. Britons suffering from pigmentosa, a degenerative eye disease, for example, can go to the Camilo Cienfuegos Center for procedures not available in Britain. Others come because services usually cost about half of what they do elsewhere. In 2000, rhinoplasty, or a nose job, cost $1,710 in Cuba, but $3,100 in the United States. Similarly, an abdominoplasty ("tummy tuck") cost $2,340 in Cuba, and $4,198 in the United States.

Celebrities escape to Cuba to avoid the media scrutiny they are often subjected to, though their presence hardly ever goes unnoticed. In January 2000, the Argentine former soccer star Diego Maradona arrived for drug treatment after suffering a heart attack while vacationing in Punta del Este, Uruguay. Warned by his doctor that any ingestion of controlled substances would kill him, Maradona agreed to go to Cuba, where, after tests in Havana, he checked into El

Quinqué, in Holguín, a city some 700 kilometers east of the capital. Built in the late 1980s, this drug rehabilitation clinic offers luxurious (by Cuban standards) amenities, including swimming pool and gym, for fifty clients at a time. Aside from a few well-publicized altercations with the press during the first days of his stay in Cuba, all else seems to have pleased Maradona. He remained at El Quinqué for two years. In 2004, when he was once again undergoing drug treatment, he asked to be transferred from an Argentine clinic to El Quinqué in Cuba.

Left turns

The continual reinvention of the revolution has coincided with the re-emergence of the left in Latin America. Not only is Cuba adjusting to a changing world, the world is changing in relation to Cuba. Soon after Hugo Chávez was elected to the Venezuelan presidency in 1998, he indicated that his Revolución Bolivariana would embrace Fidel Castro's Cuban revolution. Chávez had already visited Cuba in 1994 and traveled again to Havana in January 1999, just after his inauguration. In both policy and political style, Chávez exhibited left-leaning, populist tendencies and pitted himself against US hegemony and neoliberalism. Domestically, he created programs to redistribute Venezuela's oil wealth and in the process alienated the country's middle and upper classes. He launched campaigns to fight illiteracy and provide housing and food subsidies for the poor. With the support of the military, he built clinics and rebuilt roads. He used his considerable media skills and charismatic presence very effectively, particularly in a weekly television and radio program, *Hello President*, which he hosts. More ambivalent about liberal democracy, he has set up popular assemblies while at the same time asserting authoritarian control over the legislative and judicial branches of the state and silencing opposition. He has been accused of cronyism and corruption and squandering the country's considerable oil revenues. Growing opposition culminated in a coup attempt in 2002 that forced him to leave the country. After his triumphant return two days later, the opposition lost momentum. Despite ongoing strikes and protests, he has emerged the winner in a 2004 recall vote and the 2006 elections.

From the beginning, Chávez actively and publicly forged an alliance with Fidel Castro. After his initial visit as president in 1999, he returned eight times in five years. The two leaders linked their nations on many different levels, from baseball to petroleum. Exchange programs began in earnest. Soon busloads of Venezuelan students crowded Havana's streets. They attended special sessions at the University of Havana to learn about Bolívar and Bolivarismo, which is at the center of Chávez's vision for Latin America.

At the official level, Castro and Chávez established the Alternativo Bolivariano para las Américas (Bolivarian Alternative for the Americas) or ALBA, a trade agreement between the two countries that gave each country preferential access to the other's markets. Signed in November 2004, ALBA was intended to counter the Free Trade Agreement of the Americas, proposed by the United States, and includes financing by Venezuelan banks of Venezuelan exporters and Cuban importers. Products imported to Cuba from other countries were replaced by Venezuelan goods. These were mostly products of small industries: laboratory supplies, footwear, clothing, and bedding, among others. Tariff barriers between the two countries disappeared, and state companies could operate freely in either nation. At the heart of the agreement, however, is cheap oil for Cuba in exchange for assistance with public health programs for Venezuela. Venezuela sells about 53,000 barrels daily at discount, meeting about 25 per cent of Cuba's oil needs. In 2005/06, 15,000 Cuban doctors traveled to Venezuela to participate in "Misión Barrio Adentro," a program specifically targeting lower-income Venezuelans. This campaign has received its share of criticism, most notably from the Venezuelan Medical Federation, which sponsored protests in 2005, accusing the Cuban doctors of taking away their jobs.

Venezuela has also emulated Cuba's efforts to provide aid to other Latin American and Caribbean nations. In the aftermath of the hurricanes of 2004, the Venezuelan government shipped boatloads of building supplies and construction equipment to the worst-hit areas of the Caribbean, including Cuba, Jamaica, Haiti, and Grenada, to assist reconstruction efforts. Dubbed the Apoyo Naval Humanitario a los Hermanos del Caribe (Humanitarian Naval Assistance for Brothers of the Caribbean), the expedition, in addition to providing much-needed aid, also advertised the benevolence of Hugo Chávez's regime. When Fidel Castro boarded one of the ships and praised the project, he rhetorically envisioned himself and Chávez as the Caribbean's two caretakers and benefactors. Hardly the needy victims of a new world order, Castro and Chávez have fashioned themselves into regional leaders. Whether the rest of Latin America will follow is yet to be determined.

One nation that has recently joined the ALBA alliance is Bolivia. When Evo Morales was elected in December 2005, he declared provocatively: "long live coca, down with the Yankees."[9] On his first trip abroad after his victory, he traveled to Cuba to invite Fidel Castro to his inauguration. Their meeting on that occasion lasted seventeen hours. Morales gave Castro a miner's helmet, and they exchanged compliments. Castro stated, "the map seems to be changing," referring to the election of Morales; at a later meeting, Morales called Castro "the grandfather who guides and directs us."[10]

Concrete arrangements also emerged from this visit. In January, Cuba and Bolivia signed an agreement to stamp out illiteracy and promote cooperation in sports, health, and culture. Cuba offered to provide eye operations to 50,000 Bolivians a year and university scholarships to 5,000 students. Just five months later Bolivia opened the fourth of six planned ophthalmology clinics funded and built by the Cubans. In part, these exchanges continued a long-standing practice of Cuban assistance to Bolivia, even during periods when the governments were not as ideologically in tune as after Morales's election. But the rituals of friendship between Castro and Morales have become much more pronounced. Although it never materialized, Morales's promise of a cake of coca leaves for the Cuban leader's birthday on 13 August 2006 suggests a certain self-consciousness about the performance. This dance includes Chávez as well. The three were seen together quite often, and seldom parted without warm hugs. The countries have formed an alternative bloc, their leaders (Morales, Chávez and Lage) meeting in Vienna as an alternative to the summit taking place among officials of the United States, Latin America, and the Caribbean. Morales formally signed up to ALBA in April 2006.

Left behind

Different sectors in the United States have noticed that Cuba has initiated its economic recovery and is receiving support and assistance from Latin America. Their response has been multivocal. As the Bush administration has tried to crack down, American business, oil, and agriculture interests are clamoring for a share of the market. This two-sided approach offers a new variation on the complex theme of Cuba's relationship with the United States over the past forty-five years. Their mutual animosity and hostile gestures have propped one another up over the years, for the conflict became a source of legitimacy. Since the relationship is asymmetrical, this has been more true for Cuba than for the United States.

The 1960 Cuban expropriation of American property, the disastrous 1961 Bay of Pigs invasion, and the 1962 Cuban missile crisis set the stage for the rupture between the United States and Cuba. The USA imposed an embargo incrementally, beginning with a ban on all exports to Cuba, except for food and medicine, in 1960. After the Bay of Pigs, a ban on imports from Cuba followed. In 1963 the US government, invoking the Trading with the Enemy Act, froze all Cuban assets in the United States. Finally, in 1964 the Commerce Department revoked the license permitting the export of food and medicine. Facing the hardships of the mid-1960s and early 1970s, Cubans demonstrated great revolutionary fervor and loyalty.

A brief relaxation under the presidency of Jimmy Carter, during which travel restrictions were loosened and interest sections as the only diplomatic channels opened in both countries, came to a grinding halt after the election of Ronald Reagan in 1980. Reagan banned US business and tourist travel to Cuba, founded Radio Martí, which broadcasts anti-Castro messages from Miami, and reduced the amount Cubans in the USA could send to their families in Cuba in remittances.

The 1992 Cuban Democracy Act added still more restrictions. It forbade foreign subsidiaries of US companies from doing business in Cuba, demanded that ships docking in Cuban harbors wait 180 days before entering US waters, and called for an end to aid to any country that provided assistance to Cuba. Coming at a time of deteriorating economic conditions for Cuba, the act furnished ammunition for the government claims that it was under siege, that sacrifices would be necessary, and that efforts to open up the economy, however distasteful, were imperative. That same year Cuba loosened its regulations on foreign investment to permit, for the first time, foreign investment in the form of joint ventures. It also passed a law to prevent US subsidiaries in Cuba from complying with the Cuban Democracy Act.

In this historical context, the Helms-Burton Act of 1996 appears mainly a reaffirmation of previous policies. It allows Americans with claims to expropriated property to sue foreign corporations in charge of that property and sanctions the denial of entry to executives of those companies. The law also authorized waivers of these provisions, which Clinton implemented throughout his presidency. But this has had mixed results, with corporations and countries already beginning to take advantage of Cuba's gestures to encourage foreign investment. Although some countries did drop their plans for investment, others defiantly continued to do business with Cuba. Such extensions of the embargo actually benefited foreign companies by freeing them from American competition, and gave Cubans an external target for their frustrations.

Cuba's modest economic turnaround has initiated a new stage in US–Cuban relations. The Office of Foreign Assets Control, which issues licenses to US citizens to spend dollars in Cuba, has grown more restrictive in the last five years. Undoubtedly attentive to both federal and local pressures, the Florida legislature has recently prohibited scholars at state universities from using even non-state funds to travel to Cuba. While George Bush's Commission to Free Cuba urged the strict enforcement of the Helms-Burton Act, there are clear signs of political fragmentation over Cuba. Representative Charles Rangel's amendment proposing an end to the embargo gains more votes each year, but has yet to pass. At the same time, the Florida contingent in the House of Representatives remains firmly anti-Castro.

More surprising are the divisions emerging among traditionally conservative business groups. Exporters of food and medicine find Cuba a potentially lucrative market worth approximately $800 million a year. Yet Treasury Department regulations continue to throw up obstacles, most recently to deny credit to Cuban importers, requiring them to pay in cash. Once Soviet subsidies disappeared, American agricultural producers saw potential new markets for their products. Pressure from agriculture lobbies, many from the pre-dominantly Republican Midwest, has led to a proposed amendment to overturn trade restrictions.

No less vociferous are American oil companies clamoring for a chance to bid on oil exploration rights in Cuban waters. Since Cuba opened its reserves to outsiders in 1990, oil firms from countries like Norway, India, Canada, and Brazil have begun exploration. US oil companies now want to join the "oil rush." In 2006 legislators introduced the Western Hemisphere Security Act to alter the embargo to allow oil companies to explore Cuba's waters. There is no guarantee, of course, that Cuba would accept US bids, when it has already signed deals with other countries whose work seems to be proceeding well. Observers predict that the continuing thirst for oil in the United States will eventually demolish decades of barriers to US–Cuban trade relations. At the same time, strengthening ties between Cuba and other countries with considerable resources, such as Venezuela and China, have created the conditions in which Cuba can carry on despite the embargo, rendering it less effective with every passing day.

All these changes have considerably attenuated the influence of anti-Castro Cuban exiles. In the 1980s, following Ronald Reagan's election, their influence peaked. The Cuban American National Foundation, known for its energetic and vociferous opposition to Castro, was created in 1980 as the established exile community sought to distinguish themselves from the less prosperous Cubans who arrived in the wake of the Mariel crisis. They have been instrumental in supporting Cuban-American politicians who have worked at both the local and federal levels for tougher anti-Castro policies. But the maintenance of the embargo and the Helms-Burton Act only stiffened Cuba's resolve to seek alternatives beyond the United States. Its success in circumventing the US-imposed obstacles has to a certain extent defanged Castro's Miami opponents.

At the same time, the next generation has not necessarily followed in their footsteps. Many sons and daughters have rebelled against the older generation by adopting a more sympathetic stance towards the revolution, resenting the prohibitions against traveling there, and as children of the prosperous so often do, leaning to the left. As sociologist Alejandro Portes observed, by the early 1990s the once solidary Cuban-American community "frayed at the edges" and began to speak with many voices rather than just one.[11]

Conclusion

When the Soviet Union imploded and socialism collapsed in eastern Europe, Cuba lost billions of dollars in yearly subsidies, and three-quarters of its foreign trade. Longtime observers of Cuba predicted the end of the regime, and the economic crisis that brought frightening levels of scarcity and culminated in the riots in the summer of 1994 seemed to reinforce the fragile and faltering nature of one of the last remaining socialist regimes on earth. But Cuba has recovered. It has done so with a unique combination of commitment to revolution and reinvention of its relationship to global markets. This has produced some contradictions. A new class of consumers can afford satellite dishes, fancy *quinceañera* parties for their daughters' fifteenth birthdays, and fax machines. At the same time campaigns to rouse nationalism and commitment to the revolution, such as the efforts to bring Elián González back and the attention given to the Cuban Five, remind Cubans that they are still in a revolution. From an outside perspective, the embargo has reduced the competition for non-US investors, while in the United States oil and agriculture companies find themselves aligned with the traditional left in opposition to the embargo. Cuba has somehow simultaneously opened to market forces and posed as leader of the rising opposition to neoliberalism in Latin America. All this has also made the art of prediction increasingly risky.

3 | The traffic

If Haitians were looking forward to a Duvalier-free future in 1986 and Cubans were unknowingly about to embark on controversial reforms that would ultimately save the revolutionary regime, Jamaicans were undergoing a very different transition. The mid-1980s marked a turning point as a shift from one principal commodity to another transformed drug trafficking and consumption. In the 1960s Jamaican law enforcement and "respectable" Jamaicans worked to restrain and reform Rastafarians who smoked ganja, shunned politics, and tuned out of society. Marijuana had been introduced long before, but its use had been limited to domestic consumption. By the 1970s, marijuana had become a major commodity, marketed to thousands of users in Europe and the Americas. Jamaicans abroad had come to control the marijuana traffic from their island, a large share of the total traffic flowing from the Caribbean and South America. By the mid-1980s, however, marijuana was overtaken by cocaine in global markets, and though Jamaicans did not produce cocaine they participated in the trade, which eventually moved through the Caribbean as well. Some estimates say that as much as 40 per cent of the cocaine and crack that goes to the United States is controlled by Jamaican groups. Jamaicans everywhere were focusing on the corruption and violence associated with cocaine dealers, posses, and traffickers who were not consumers or producers but movers of a lucrative commodity, with close connections to worldwide networks, access to high-tech communication and, some say, well-placed officials and politicians.

This is a tale of two substances and of their changing fortunes in a changing world. Jamaica has an unusual relationship to these substances. First there was ganja (Hindi for cannabis or marijuana), introduced to Jamaica in the mid-nineteenth century and cultivated there ever since, mainly for local consumption. Then there was cocaine, not native to Jamaica, but whose shipment through Jamaica has steadily increased since the 1980s, affecting the lives of many in the process. There are not many places that have felt the impact of all three aspects of the circulation of drugs: production, consumption, and transshipment.

This is also a tale of secrets and lies, of fragmentary and hidden information, of relationships and networks that will only ever partially be known. The nature of drug production and trafficking is such that the sources come from law enforcement, whose information is necessarily incomplete, or from the participants themselves, who have reasons to focus on some aspects and hide others. Knowledge about the drug trade is necessarily partial, but it is nonetheless possible to get a glimpse of a process that includes many lives and shapes them in important ways.

My strategy in this complex story will be to investigate the many connections made through the circulation of drugs. This will take the narrative back in time, to convey a sense of drug consumption and circulation as dependent on political and social contingency rather than predisposition to addiction. It also takes the narrative away from Jamaica at times, following the traffickers to their various sites of operation. But if one of the central arguments of this book is that the Caribbean is connected to the wider world in important ways, then the stories must encompass a broad geographical scope. I do not argue that all Jamaicans are drug traffickers. What I do argue is that the large scale of drug traffic has shaped Jamaican society and politics in important ways, especially in the last twenty years. It has also shaped the United States, Colombia, Peru, the Netherlands, and many other places. Here I try to tell the particular story of Jamaica as a phenomenon that cannot be ignored. The chapter weaves the accounts of the very different impacts of two different drugs, shifting scales from the individual to the societal and geopolitical, in an effort to show how these lucrative substances flow at various levels.

How ganja came to Jamaica

When slavery was abolished in Jamaica in 1838, plantation owners faced the problem of persuading former slaves to continue to do the work they had been doing. Sugar plantations needed to be operating, households needed to be run, livestock needed to be tended, and urban dwellers needed all the services and crafts that urban slaves had come to provide. But many former slaves were not interested in wage labor. They wanted greater control over their lives and hence retreated to the woods and took up subsistence farming. The search for new workers brought an influx of indentured laborers from India, recently colonized by the British. From 1838 until 1917, just over half a million workers came to the Caribbean from India. While both British Guiana and Trinidad took in greater numbers, some 36,000 Indians ended up in Jamaica. They brought with them ganja, a plant whose cultivation was essential for both medicinal and spiritual purposes. It was used to cure illnesses like colds and flu and brewed in healthful tea. The plant served ritual and recreational purposes as well. Barry Chevannes, who has written extensively on the cultivation and use of cannabis in Jamaica, notes that as recently as 1971, among people of East Indian descent, "ganja smoking was an afterwork recreational activity, pursued in conjunction with the heavy drinking of white rum and stout, and amidst the singing of Hindi songs to the music of the saranggi (violin), the manjara (bell), and the dolak (drum), the recounting of stories, or the racing of cardboard 'horses' in the gutter after a shower of rain."[1] Since there were fewer workers in Jamaica than in British Guiana or Trinidad, they were more likely to intermingle with Jamaicans of African descent who toiled alongside them. Thus the use of ganja spread beyond the ethnic boundary and became a common practice in Jamaican society. When, in the early nineteenth century, Jamaicans traveled to Central America to work on the Panama Canal and in the growing banana industry, they made sure to bring adequate quantities of ganja with them.

Perceptions of the effects of ganja use underwent a dramatic transformation in the early twentieth century. Noticing the widespread use of ganja, also known as hemp, in India, the British government formed a commission to investigate the possible deleterious effects of smoking hemp. The Indian Hemp Drug Commission issued its report in 1894 in seven volumes. It concluded that moderate smoking was neither harmful to health nor a source of criminal activity or mental disorders. It was a short-lived reprieve.

By 1912 Jamaican authorities were concerned enough about the dangers of ganja to join the Hague Opium Convention of that year and add the plant to the latter's list of opiates. This agreement, signed by officials from many countries, including Great Britain, France, China, Japan, and the United States, came out of a conference convened by the United States in 1909, to deal with growing anxieties about the opium trade primarily from China. Although the signatories intended to suppress the use of opium, morphine, and cocaine, not until the Dangerous Drugs Act of 1924 did these prohibitions receive backing from law enforcement agencies. Of particular interest to Jamaica, the act set penalties for the cultivation, trafficking, possession, and smoking of marijuana. The increasing harshness of these penalties in the years that followed reflected both an international trend towards the criminalization of narcotic and psychotropic substances and changing patterns of use within Jamaica itself.

The rise of cocaine

Cocaine has a long global history. The first recorded processing of coca leaf into cocaine took place in 1860 in a German laboratory with coca leaves from Peru. Soon chemists, physicians, and pharmacists began to research its effects and potential uses. When its anesthetic qualities were discovered, interest peaked and uses multiplied. Until the turn of the century, cocaine was a legal ingredient in a variety of products, including health tonics, toothache remedies, hemorrhoid ointments, lozenges and, of course, Coca-Cola. It was hailed as a miracle drug that would energize, sharpen, numb, or revive mind and body.

Located mainly in Germany, the Netherlands, and the United States, the laboratories initially imported dried leaf directly from Peru. After 1885, however, Peru also began to process its coca leaf, producing semi-refined cocaine for export and further refinement in the United States and Europe, the largest consumers of the drug. In Peru, cocaine was a miracle not for its perceived medical benefits but for its boost to an ailing economy in post-independence doldrums. Economic modernizers hoped that the success of the cocaine industry would ripple through the society and propel it into a new phase marked by science, efficiency, and technological innovation.

Even as levels of consumption were rising, or perhaps because they were rising, critics began to worry about the dangers of ingesting cocaine and the potential for addiction. Between 1900 and 1920, their mounting attacks would eventually demonize cocaine and lead to a series of prohibitionist measures. For many, addiction threatened both physical and mental health in the United States. Not only were cocaine addicts frenetic and emaciated, but they also suffered from hallucinations and psychotic or obsessive behavior. In London, cocaine was linked to a world of prostitution and gambling that could undermine middle-class values. In Germany, the pharmaceutical industry's increasing fragmentation combined with bureaucratic maneuvering among German ministries brought that country on to the prohibitionist bandwagon.

The 1912 agreement thus began the process of driving cocaine underground by the 1920s. As cocaine became illicit, levels of consumption and trafficking rose in the Caribbean. Americans escaping prohibition in the 1920s and 1930s traveled to Cuba to take advantage of widely circulating recreational drugs as well as free-flowing liquor. Cubans began to traffic in cocaine, exploiting their contacts with the US Mafia, which controlled a great deal of the gambling and alcohol distribution in Cuba at the time. But by the 1950s cocaine consumption had diminished everywhere, owing to US efforts and Peru's eventual compliance. After the Cuban revolution in 1959, drug trafficking all but disappeared there as well. Not until the 1970s did the drug return as the jet-setters' choice drug. In this phase, Colombia took over production, and the Caribbean once again entered the story as a way station in the flow of drugs to the United States and Europe.[2]

Popular politics and the culture of ganja

By the 1970s in Jamaica, marijuana had acquired new meanings as a consequence of cultural and political transformations dating back to the 1930s, as the evolving practice of Rastafarianism came to be intimately linked with smoking marijuana. Rastafarianism began following the 1930 coronation of Ethiopian emperor Haile Selassie

I, also known as Ras Tafari Makonnen. The Rastafari believed in the divinity of this emperor, and hence called for the repatriation of all Africans and condemned colonialism. Smoking ganja and letting their hair grow as dreadlocks are often the only Rastafarian practices known to the wider public. Yet these were not embraced by most Rastafarians until the 1960s, when several confrontations with the Jamaican police served to crystallize Rastafarianism as an oppositional ideology. No longer confined to small groups, it spread throughout poor neighborhoods in urban Jamaica. When the rising stars of reggae, most notably Bob Marley, adopted Rastafarianism in public and in private, its appeal spread worldwide, as did that of his music.

In 1972, just as Bob Marley released *Catch a Fire*, his first record with the British label Island Records, Jamaicans voted the People's National Party into office. Its leader and now prime minister Michael Manley came from an activist family. His father Norman Manley, along with his cousin Alexander Bustamante, had been central to the emergence of party politics on the island in the 1930s and 1940s. During this period of trade union struggles and mounting demands for inclusion by the black majority, each of these men founded his own party: Bustamante the Jamaican Labour Party (JLP) and Manley the People's National Party (PNP). With contrasting styles – Manley an England-educated member of the mulatto elite; Bustamante an oft-described "near-white" from a working-class background with a populist charismatic appeal – but similar political strategies and goals, they ushered Jamaicans into independence and decolonization. Together they imbued Jamaican politics with the populist, clientelistic flavor it carries to this day.

After independence in 1962, Jamaican politics were shaped, as many island nations are, by the constraints of an economy dependent on one or two major exports – largely bauxite in the case of Jamaica. But Jamaica also held on to its traditions of labor activism and popular participation in electoral politics. It navigated these currents and the growing influence of international lending agencies like the IMF and the World Bank with varying degrees of state intervention in the economy and attempts to generate economic growth. The PNP years of Michael Manley (1972–80) are remembered as a period of democratic socialism, during which the government worked to place foreign investors under the watchful eye of the state, and to redistribute wealth and provide social services. This economic populism came with other, more symbolic gestures, especially to the poor.

Manley had defeated the rival JLP and their rising star Edward Seaga. Both men had wooed Jamaica's indigent and dispossessed, seeing them as crucial constituencies. In 1964, Edward Seaga of the Jamaican Labour Party brought black activist Marcus Garvey's body back to be buried in Jamaica. In 1966, the JLP hoped to shore up flagging support by inviting Haile Selassie to visit Jamaica. This appropriation or incorporation of Rastafarianism into the language of politics continued under Manley. Some people suggested this was a relationship of convenience, others a real friendship between Manley and Bob Marley. After his inauguration as prime minister, Manley was said to have spent the night at Marley's infamous Island House on Hope Road, a haunt of musicians on the fringe of respectability. The onset of PNP rule also saw the lifting of mandatory sentences for possession of marijuana dating back to amendments to the Dangerous Drugs Act in 1941. According to Barry Chevannes, this constellation of factors contributed to such a rising demand for and increased cultivation of ganja that it became a principal money crop for many small farmers. By 1980, then, cultivation and use of ganja were once again widespread.

Clientelism and the politics of violence

Both Manley and Seaga recruited the urban poor in other ways as well. They had begun to rely on the persuasive and coercive powers of neighborhood leaders to muster local support by distributing goods and jobs, and if necessary through intimidation. Many observers place the origins of gang activity, especially the turn to violence, in this emerging clientelistic context. Rumors swirled by the mid-1970s when unexplained murders, unknown gunmen, and their very well-known supporters began to make the headlines in Jamaica. Re-creating these tense times, author Laurie Gunst writes:

who was the shadowy PNP enforcer named Winston 'Burry Boy'

Blake, and why [did] Michael Manley himself choose to join Blake's funeral procession in 1975, after the gunman had been shot dead by a JLP supporter in West Kingston? ... Who were the political mercenaries who set fire to a PNP tenement yard on Orange Street one hot May night in 1976 and then shot the firefighters who tried to extinguish the blaze? ... No one dared to name **Manley or Seaga** as the men behind such outrages. Rumors flew and whispers floated from Kingston's uptown verandas. Downtown, the sufferers burned and bled.[3]

In Kingston, neighborhoods were divided into either PNP or JLP territory. In each of these, armed gangs delivered votes, distributed patronage, and intimidated the other side. Sometimes only a few hundred yards separated these zones. Everyone in these neighborhoods knew that crossing zones was a perilous endeavor. By the election season of 1976, the ubiquitous violence was so unsettling that most Jamaicans supported Manley's declaration of an emergency and subsequent arrest of almost six hundred people. Yet the 1980 election campaign turned out to be the most violent on record: over seven hundred people were murdered in the months before voters went to the polls.

The year 1980 proved to be a turning point as structural adjustment policies and austerity measures set off a chain reaction that led to migration, involvement in the international drug trade, and eventual repercussions back home. The JLP and Seaga had gained supporters and won the elections as Manley's program of increased state intervention in the economy faltered. Seaga's proposals for greater prosperity included creating a better working relationship with the United States and the international lending agencies that Manley had alienated with his determination to maintain some control over foreign investment and his friendship with Fidel Castro. Seaga's professed dislike of Castro and his promises to liberalize the economy won over Washington. Part of his plan relied on revenue from bauxite, traditionally a primary export. Unfortunately, worldwide demand for this mineral fell just as Seaga took over. He had little choice but to accept structural adjustment policies imposed by the lending agencies, which resulted in rising unemployment and diminishing social services. As Jamaicans, especially those at the lowest income levels, struggled with bleak economic realities, they adopted two related survival strategies: the informal economy and migration.

Strategies of survival

Like Haitians, Jamaicans have been migrating and circulating within the Caribbean and beyond for over a century. They followed the demands of the labor market, especially to the Panama Canal and the Central American banana boom. But they also worked on Costa Rican railroads and Cuban sugar plantations until the depression of the 1930s contracted labor markets everywhere. Jamaicans returned home, either by choice or, as occurred in Cuba, because of a nationalist repatriation campaign to send all foreign workers back to their countries of origin. After World War II, Jamaicans traveled to Canada, the United Kingdom, and the United States. In Britain, they rebuilt decimated cities and filled positions left open by the generation of young men who went off to fight and did not return. With Canadian and American immigration restrictions lifted, newcomers established ties with existing communities. In Canada, many West Indians ended up in Toronto and Montreal. In the United States, most Jamaicans went to New York or Boston, remaining primarily on the east coast. Because many Jamaicans traveled on British passports, precise numbers are difficult to obtain.

Starting in 1980, Jamaica's declining economy spurred a continued emigration to all parts of the world. Since Edward Seaga's administration wanted stronger ties to the United States, he encouraged emigration in that direction. At the same time, newly elected Ronald Reagan was eager to support Seaga since the JLP leader had from his first days in office established himself as generally anticommunist and specifically anti-Castro. In return he became the first head of state to visit the White House after Reagan's inauguration. Reagan encouraged migration by making it easier for Jamaicans to obtain visas. Between 1980 and 1990, 213,805 Jamaicans traveled to the United States, a dramatic 9 per cent of the population. Like other migrant groups, they created new lives for themselves in diverse ways. Many entered numerous occupations as part of the working class but aspired to more. They placed great emphasis on education and urged their children to attend university. Others, especially young unemployed men, had worked for Seaga as "enforcers" or "gunmen" who relied on violence as one of several methods to maintain party loyalty in their Jamaican neighborhoods. Once they had relocated to the United States, they found ways to use their skills and networks as they were drawn into increasingly lucrative drug smuggling.

Dealers needed

At this point the Jamaican chronicle of economic struggles, party politics, and emigration becomes entangled with the North American story of rising drug consumption, the War on Drugs, and deteriorating urban landscapes. Under President Reagan, the War on Drugs helped globalize the drug trade by focusing on drug production and transshipment, much of which occurred beyond US borders. Reagan almost doubled the budget from $1.5 billion in 1981 to $2.75 billion in 1986 and shifted attention to the international arena. One of the many campaigns that formed part of the War on Drugs involved the attempted eradication of marijuana plots in both Colombia and Jamaica. Most accounts credit this program with unforeseen "successes" – not in reducing total production or consumption but rather in transforming the nature of cultivation and export. Early on, the eradication campaign managed to cut off the supply from Colombia. Jamaicans stepped in almost immediately and began to smuggle and sell their marijuana. Many recent emigrants from political gangs reorganized in the USA as "posses," using their political leverage and tightly knit networks to break in to trafficking.

Bringing in marijuana was a lucrative venture: the price of one pound in Jamaica was $20, while in North America dealers could get up to $1,200 for it. Some estimates claim that by the mid-1980s Jamaican profits from the marijuana trade were twice those of bauxite, agriculture, and manufacturing combined. Once it discovered the source of this new marijuana supply, the United States forced Seaga to crack down on the trade. He responded by destroying airstrips, enlisting the military to oversee airports, firing many airport personnel, and pursuing the major traffickers. The flood of marijuana from

Jamaica abated. Localized cultivation of marijuana in the United States and Canada took off precisely during this period.

Cocaine returns

At the same time cocaine was replacing marijuana as the substance of choice. In the case of cocaine, consumption took place mostly in the United States and Europe. By the early 1980s cocaine had seduced 9 million users in the United States. Consumption levels remained this high through the mid-1990s. In the early years of the "boom" the high prices of cocaine restricted its use mostly to upper and upper-middle classes. Cocaine became part of an urban lifestyle of extravagant consumption. Popular culture from that era oozes with the clichés of a fast, dangerous, moneyed world: in *Scarface* Michelle Pfeiffer's portrayal of the cocaine-addicted woman wasting away in an illicit underworld of guns, big houses, and fancy swimming pools embodied one type of iconic victim; another was the Wall Street executive who squanders his millions and alienates his friends and family in search of the ever-elusive high.

In the mid-1980s the press noted this trend and began to cover it more carefully. There are reports of the easy availability of cocaine at prep schools and colleges of the eastern establishment, whose students could afford the expense, and of secretaries stealing their grandmothers' jewelry to support their $700-a-week habits on $250-a-week salaries. Journalists, struck by the wealth and status of cocaine users, contrasted them with the marijuana smokers of the 1970s, whose drug use frequently advertised an anti-establishment ideology. Cocaine users, on the contrary, seemed mostly overachievers deeply invested in "the system."

The press also discussed the introduction of crack cocaine, a crystallized form of the powder produced by cooking it with baking soda. Some accounts traced the origin of this version to the Bahamas, another transshipment center. Cocaine use in the Bahamas itself, so the story goes, increased so much that people eventually grew bored with it, so they invented crack as a new way to get high. This high is much more intense, but shorter, leaving users craving more. Since crack was cheaper than pure cocaine, it quickly spread among the less affluent. Inner cities became the epicenters of the "crack epidemic." Crack increased street violence as users committed robberies and dealers struggled to gain control of particular markets.

In this second round of cocaine's popularity, Colombians came to control the trade. Before that, drugs had been transported by either Cuban or Chilean traffickers. The Cuban revolution led to many traffickers moving to the USA, however, and especially Miami, while the 1973 Chilean coup led by General Augusto Pinochet brought an end to drug trafficking there. Colombians stepped in and began to move drugs with increasing success. They also began to refine coca from Peru and Bolivia, becoming producers as well as shippers.

This was the era of the notorious "drug lords" such as Pablo Escobar, known to be ruthless with his enemies, but also remembered in Medellín as a benefactor and patron who distributed groceries, installed lights in playgrounds so that children could play soccer at night, and offered employment and aid to many Colombians at a time of great need. He could afford to be generous. The drug smuggling business earned him and his rivals in Cali $7 to $12 billion a year.

During this time drugs were transported mostly through Mexico and Florida. In 1981 Florida was one of the main points of entry, with an estimated 70 per cent of the marijuana and cocaine headed for US markets passing through its ports and shores. Networks of Colombians who had been migrating to the USA since the 1960s participated in the trade. Drugs also passed through the lengthy Mexico–US border, which is nearly impossible to control.

Jamaicans might have been left out of the loop of drug trafficking as marijuana use dropped and cocaine use rose, but posses were determined not to lose their position as prominent traffickers. Jamaican posses soon joined the ranks of major dealers of crack and cocaine. As the most prominent of these drug-trafficking posses, named Shower and Spangler, consolidated and came to control greater shares of the drug trade, they became more visible to the American public and the media. By cleverly combining legitimate business practices with tightly monitored loyalty and the occasional spectacular act of violence, they controlled most aspects of drug shipment, distribution, and sales. Using cell phones and rental cars to avoid detection, they picked up cocaine at delivery points in New York or Miami and then fanned out across the country to oversee the processing of cocaine into crack and to control the crack houses where it was sold. Almost everyone involved in the network was of Jamaican origin. While many of the players eschewed flashy consumerism and lived in low-income neighborhoods without drawing attention to themselves, others happily bathed in the spotlight of the cars, the clothing, and especially, the guns. While initially sticking to traditional Jamaican communities like Miami, New York, and Washington, they eventually spread out. Students of gangs and violence have traced them to Dallas, Chicago, Kansas City, Cleveland, Denver, Rochester, Boston, and Buffalo.

Most depictions of Jamaican gangs focus on their penchant for extreme and ostentatious acts of violence. Laurie Gunst's book *Born Fi' Dead*, recognized for its complex rendition of gang life, includes, alongside humanizing and fascinating portraits, many accounts of murders and beatings. In a widely remembered incident in 1985, gunmen opened fire on picnicking Jamaicans in a New Jersey park. Quick-tempered posse dons have been accused of murdering policemen, their own associates, or passers-by who happened to annoy them – all this often in public and in broad daylight.

Flows and interdictions

Repercussions from the fall of communism in 1989 drew Colombian and Jamaican traffickers closer together. Reacting to the end of the cold war, Bush planned to cut the military budget, since many of the programs in place would no longer be necessary. Less money for all military operations would mean less money for the War on Drugs. But Colombian developments changed that trajectory. When the assassination of a presidential candidate in August 1989 set off a new terrorism campaign by traffickers opposed to extradition, the US military realized that its participation in this conflict might justify continuing its level of funding. The increased militarization of drug combating efforts, including the sale of military equipment and the use of US personnel for assistance and training, was the result of a changing economy of conflict, fear, and rationalization.

Traffickers responded to increasingly sophisticated efforts at drug interdiction in kind. They improved forms of communication, up-graded transportation, and changed strategies. They began to use many entry points instead of a few, to transport drugs in smaller shipments, and to track their trackers. When the focus on points of entry in Florida and Mexico intensified, traffickers discovered the Caribbean's many advantages. It offered numerous small bays where operations could go unnoticed, suffered from an understaffed and underpaid police force, and allowed for modes of transport that could easily elude the authorities. The death of Pablo Escobar in 1993 and the disintegration of his Medellín cartel provided further impetus for this shift. Smaller and dispersed competing groups took the place of one dominant organization in control of most of the trafficking.

US drug enforcement agents have over the last decade concentrated on what they call "supply reduction," a strategy that targets the places of origin in an effort to reduce the supply of drugs before it reaches the United States. Despite bringing billions of dollars in aid to Colombia, this, for most observers, has actually increased the supply of cocaine. As criminologist Marlyn Jones wrote in 2002, "coca cultivation has expanded, efficiency in extracting cocaine from the coca leaf has increased, and narco-political alliances have been strengthened."[4] Shifting smuggling routes to the Caribbean thus allowed cocaine traffic to continue to grow in spite of intense interdiction efforts.

In 2000, the *International Narcotics Control Strategy Report*, produced by the US government, identified Jamaica as a major transit point for cocaine originating in South America. According to US customs, the majority of passengers found with drugs in US airports flew from Jamaica. Between 1999 and 2001, the amount of cocaine passing through Jamaica increased fourfold. Colombian suppliers control the cocaine entering Jamaica, while groups from the Bahamas provide what Jones calls "navigational services," and locals supply knowledge of smuggling routes and methods. Cocaine moves through the Caribbean in diverse ways. Recent years have seen the adoption of smaller, slower "go boats," because they are much harder to detect. The use of mules – people who smuggle cocaine by ingesting small bags of it – has also increased. In the Jamaican case, they are usually women on flights to the United States or Europe, despite the serious risk of death and the high rates of detection. In 2003, British authorities arrested at least one Jamaican woman daily for smuggling drugs this way, with the number of female Jamaicans in British jails soaring to 700 in the recent past.

Crack goes to Europe

Crack hit England somewhat later than it did the United States. While never attaining the epidemic proportions of its American consumption, crack spread through the cities and altered the British drug scene. The lucrative returns of this trade – one could make £10,000–20,000 a week – attracted Jamaican dealers, known in Britain as Yardies or Rude Boys. As dealers began to steal drugs from one another and to protect their territories more aggressively, they contributed to the general escalation of violent crime in London and elsewhere in the late 1980s and early 1990s. Geoff Small's *Ruthless* describes shootings like the one in August 1988, when an all-night dance became the scene of a gun battle with ten rounds of ammunition fired. Despite the use of multiple firearms in a crowded place, prosecution proved difficult. Witnesses were too terrified to speak. Small talks of a new level of intimidation: "experienced, ruthless and fearless gunmen, they were the trend-setters for black Britain's current nightmare of violent and gun-toting crime. They legitimized the mundane carrying of illegal firearms, they introduced the concept of drive-by shootings, public execution-style slayings … they made it acceptable to shoot at unarmed police officers and innocent passers by." Small lingers on the cruelty of such Rude Boys pastimes as throwing naked women out of windows or spraying bullets indiscriminately at passers-by and targeted victims alike in a drive-by.[5]

Crack quickly spread to other cities, including Bristol, Nottingham, Manchester, Birmingham, and Leeds. In response, British police stepped up enforcement, intensified undercover work, and adopted controversial measures like carrying unconcealed weapons. Arrest rates and drug seizures did increase. But, as in the United States, there was also abuse and mistreatment of suspects, epitomized by the strip search of a female suspect on a street corner.

Effects at home

These far-flung developments had domestic repercussions. The 1980s escalation of drug trafficking occurred just as the Jamaican government adopted neoliberal policies, initiated structural adjustments, and reduced state spending. Those residents of marginal neighborhoods who did not choose to leave during this period experienced the litany of unhappy effects of government constraints on social spending. Social programs in education and public employment were cut by 44 per cent between 1981 and 1985. At the neighborhood level, the effects of these changes interfered with local politicians' abilities to distribute patronage, which they relied on to sustain loyalty. As the traditional power brokers in these neighborhoods, political parties found their influence diminished.[6]

This provided an opening for drug "dons" to take over the patronage networks the government was forced to abandon. The profits they had made in dealings abroad allowed them to dominate Kingston neighborhoods at home. Some of these leaders acquired reputations as generous benefactors. Numerous accounts of Jim Brown's funeral, for example, emphasize the grief of the thousands who attended. Persistent memories of the jobs, housing, and protection these leaders provided testify that they, like Medellín drug lords, built and maintained strong networks of reciprocal and often mutually beneficial relationships. In Small's view, members of the "Spanglers posse form the ghetto government of the Matthews Lane precinct. They are the leading industrialists, social carers, security forces, lawmakers, judges, juries and jailors. And their members are folk heroes and role models for many a wannabe gangster."[7] This shift occurred with a price, however, as more money meant the replacement of handguns with semiautomatic weapons and submachine guns. Jamaican police began to uncover large stockpiles of the weapons in various parts of the island. The violence that had been driven by political parties turned into violence led by drug gangs as battles over turf, loyalty, and revenge killings continued.

One paradoxical effect of the state's abandonment of neighborhoods and their patronage networks was a growing critique of political parties and the status quo. As the state was increasingly perceived to be ineffective, a number of groups in civil society began to express their dissatisfaction. In addition, they formed non-partisan associations and organizations to provide education and training to neighborhood residents and counter some of the worst effects of constrained social spending. While power was once tightly controlled by the rival political parties, their weakening meant the strengthening of alternatives. Drug traffickers were at an advantage in some ways because of their extensive resources. But other groups filled the vacuum left by fading party influence as well. The combined result of heightened drug traffic and pressure to implement neoliberal policies fragmented power in Jamaica, changing the political landscape in profound ways.

But this is a tale of two substances, and the plotline for marijuana is quite different from that of cocaine. A 1990 survey of drug use in Jamaica found the smoking of marijuana quite widespread but varying according to gender, age, and locale. In urban metropolitan areas, 47 per cent of the men stated they had smoked marijuana at some point in their lives while 30 per cent said that they currently used the drug. Of women, 17 per cent said they had used it but only 4 per cent were current users. In rural areas the numbers were slightly lower. Overall, active ganja users totaled about 9 per cent of the entire population.[8] The study concluded that while in the 1970s the use of ganja was restricted to the less privileged and Rastafarians, by 1990, the date of the survey, it had infiltrated the upper classes as well and formed "part of the lifestyle of the fast moving uptown yuppies." The same survey and many others found that a majority of Jamaicans do not think that smoking marijuana is harmful to a smoker's health or poses a social threat.

The distinctions Jamaicans draw between the violence and disruption brought on by cocaine traffic and the relatively benign domestic consumption of marijuana color their attitudes towards law enforcement. Since the Dangerous Drugs Act set jail sentences for possession of drugs, Jamaica faced overloaded courts and overcrowded prisons. Many Jamaicans stressed the futility and waste of jailing so many for minor offenses. Under pressure to differentiate among levels of drug offenses, officials implemented a number of liberalizing reforms. Among the more significant was the establishment of Drug Courts in 1999. Accepting the claims that drug abuse is a public health, not a criminal issue, the Drug Courts allow users to opt for treatment and rehabilitation rather than a prison cell. By 2003, two Drug Courts were operating in Jamaica, one in Kingston, and one in Montego Bay, a tourist center. The absence of clear intentions, however, prevented the Drug Courts from being fully effective. Although many more Jamaicans use marijuana than crack or cocaine, treatment tended to focus on crack use. Of the forty people in the rehabilitation programs soon after they began, most were being treated for crack use, and some for heroin. No one was receiving treatment for the exclusive use of marijuana. Many who entered the program dropped out before completing it. This combination of sizable dropout rates, the relatively short history of the program, and the lack of evaluative mechanisms makes it very difficult to tell how effective the Drug Courts have been in reducing demand for drugs.

Even as the Drug Courts were being established, an effort to decriminalize the use of ganja emerged. The National Commission on Ganja issued its report to Prime Minister P. J. Patterson in August 2001. The commission, whose seven members included Jamaican scholar Barry Chevannes and the Reverend Dr Webster Edwards, continued the work of an earlier committee, created in 1977, which had recommended the decriminalization of ganja for personal and medicinal uses. For nine months, the new commission gathered testimony from 400 people, making sure to include conservative groups, religious leaders and medical professionals. It also traveled throughout the island to avoid any centrist bias. In the end it concluded that most of Jamaican society supported the decriminalization of ganja for personal, medical, or spiritual use. It carefully stipulated that its recommendation did not apply to use by minors or in public places, and that decriminalization should be accompanied by campaigns to reduce drug use. Finally, it argued that law enforcers should continue to suppress large-scale ganja cultivation and trafficking of all kinds. Echoing the sentiments of many Jamaicans, it complained that while ganja merited decriminalization, crack cocaine was "ravaging urban and rural communities with addiction and corrupting otherwise productive people."[9] Although drug production, consumption, and circulation coexist alongside one another, Jamaicans are very clear about the differences between the substances.

One man's story

The life of Vivian Blake, leader of the so-called "Shower Posse" for many years, embodies the shift from marijuana to cocaine as the major trafficking drug, the transnational networks so vital to the trade, and the impact on local politics. His biography illustrates these relationships and demonstrates the ways in which participation in the drug trade meant participation in both the global economy and in neighborhood politics back in Jamaica. They are intimately connected. Blake was born in Jamaica and finished high school in 1972. While working for the PNP government, he also played cricket; and it was with his cricket team that he first visited the United States in the mid-1970s. Deciding to remain in New York, he eked out a living, working odd jobs and staying with friends and relatives. He first entered the drug world by selling marijuana, which very quickly turned profitable. With the help of a growing network of friends and family that he helped bring to the United States, he expanded his operations and was soon flying to Miami to buy marijuana shipped directly from Jamaica and distributing it to New York, Detroit, Washington DC, and Oakland. During this period he also became associated with Jim Brown, a well-known don of Tivoli Gardens, Kingston, allegedly supported by Edward Seaga. According to the biography written by his son Duane, it was during one of these trips back to Jamaica that Blake encountered cocaine, but only as a recreational drug. By the mid-1980s, however, with marijuana sales dipping, Blake began to consider switching to cocaine, which was then easier to transport and more lucrative. Using at first a connection in the Bahamas, he was soon trafficking cocaine not just in New York, but also in Los Angeles, Toronto, Philadelphia, and Baltimore.

Blake had a reputation for being an educated man with a fondness for extravagance. His biography reveals his fascination with large houses with swimming pools, BMWs, satin upholstery, and expensive champagne. He thus challenged the stereotype of the dealer as a man who came from a tougher background and kept a low profile. But his attraction to luxury did not produce a soft stance towards perceived threats or rivals.

The mid-1980s witnessed the spectacular acts of violence that earned Blake and his associates the name Shower Posse, supposedly

for the shower of bullets sprayed on their enemies in various incidents. The Shower Posse transported around 300,000 pounds of
ganja and 20,000 pounds of cocaine from Miami between 1984 and
1987. At the same time, it was also fighting for control over traffic
with the other Jamaican gang known as the Spanglers, based in Fort
Lauderdale. The combination of competing political loyalties (the
Spanglers were allegedly loyal to the PNP), a burgeoning market
for cocaine, and easy access to firearms was deadly. Dozens, if not
hundreds, died as a result.

When the authorities finally caught some of the Shower Posse and
prosecuted them in 1989, Blake and Brown were not among them.
It was not until 1994, after Blake had returned to Jamaica and taken
on the role of don of Tivoli Gardens (Brown having mysteriously died
in a prison cell), that he was finally arrested and extradited to the
United States. Some observers tie the fortunes of the Shower Posse
directly to Jamaican party politics. The year of Brown's death and
Blake's arrest coincided with the end of Seagas's regime and his
replacement by Michael Manley and the PNP. Blake was sent back
to the United States for trial shortly thereafter. He was subsequently
convicted and sentenced to twenty-eight years in prison.[10]

Ongoing battles

Jamaica's own anti-drug efforts have been guided by two five-year
plans, 1997–2002 and 2003–08. Anti-drug activity proceeds from
government agencies, such as the Ministry of Health, the Ministry
of National Security, and the Ministry of Justice. Drug issues are, of
course, only a part of each ministry's responsibilities. The Jamaican
government has seen the solution to the perceived drug problem
as one of reducing demand and supply. Efforts to lower demand
have included a series of drug abuse programs targeting what they
considered the most vulnerable sectors: students, youth no longer
at school, and workers. There are also seven walk-in centers and
six residential treatment clinics. Efforts to curtail supply are the
usual: detection, seizure and eradication by cutting down marijuana
plants.

The success of the government's eradication efforts remains hard
to gauge. Since the majority of sources are government or official

documents, we learn how many hectares the state wipes out annually. Much more difficult to discover is how many hectares remain.
Moreover, efforts at eradication have changed the nature of the
cultivation itself. Plots have shrunk from between 2 and 20 hectares
to plots of half a hectare or less to avoid detection. This has made
quantification much less precise. In 1986, a record 2,756 hectares
of cannabis were sprayed. But that year also saw twice the amount
of marijuana smuggled out of the country. Recent eradication
campaigns have proved disappointing. In 1997, 743 hectares were
eliminated, and only 209 hectares in 2000. The numbers continued
to fall dramatically in 2001. Why the rapid decline? Some think the
Jamaican government, though pressed by the US government and
international agencies, pursues these eradication campaigns half-
heartedly, because the plant is a vital source of income for many in
difficult circumstances. Related to this is the claim that the government is opposed to spraying and prefers instead to rely on the police
and military to cut down crops manually. Such a policy has stretched
an already overworked force, solely responsible for port surveillance,
and domestic crime prevention even further, to the great advantage
of marijuana cultivators and cocaine traffickers.

Recent statistics reveal increases in both traffic and in interdiction. In 2001, authorities seized 74,413 kilos of marijuana, almost
20,000 more than the previous year. Similarly, cocaine seizures rose
from 1,655 kilos of cocaine in 2000 to 2,949 kilos in 2001 and 3,261
kilos between January and September 2003. The numbers themselves can be ambiguous, however, as they cannot definitively reveal
whether a greater proportion of the traffic has been seized or whether
the flows themselves have increased over time.

Epistemology of drugs

Running through all the documents on the drug trade is the
recurrent complaint of too few and unreliable statistics. Moreover,
those who control and participate in drug trafficking have very little
interest in disclosing the details of their operations. The problems
go deeper. Even with fairly accurate statistics, questions of interpretation loom. Does an increase in the amount of drugs seized
demonstrate the success of enforcement efforts or does it merely

reflect a larger volume of traffic? But, as the documents themselves point out, illegal activity and its prosecution do not readily lend themselves to quantification. Not only is it difficult to determine how much money actually goes to drug enforcement, it has been even trickier to gauge the accuracy of data gathered to track enforcement efforts. Part of the problem is bureaucratic: information is collected by two different agencies in Jamaica and not reconciled. There are also serious gaps: for example, no attempts to evaluate the success of drug abuse treatment programs or to relate drug use with disease or mortality. The Jamaican government has not been able to determine precisely how many acres are being used for marijuana cultivation. With regard to arrests, the statistics gathered on arrests for drug violations do not distinguish between those arrested for trafficking and those arrested for possession of any amount. While the government does maintain a database of arms and weapons and their place of origin, this is not computerized, so it is not readily accessible to all enforcement agencies. Finally, there has been very little reporting of suspicious activity by banks or financial agencies. Although this is required by law, in 2000 only twenty-one such events were reported, while banking agencies reported sixty-four suspicious transactions in 2001. This resulted in no prosecutions or arrests of people for money laundering in those years. Whether these problems are due mostly to inaction, complicity, or understaffing is difficult to determine. But the opaque nature of information necessarily renders this story incomplete.

Conclusion

Marijuana arrived in Jamaica so long ago, as a by-product of global flows related to labor and colonialism, that it almost seems indigenous. It became part of cultural practice and eventually provided many with an important source of income during times of economic crisis. Although it is acknowledged to have become part of the global trade linking drugs with violence, its domestic consumption is widely defended. The introduction of cocaine, a foreign substance which very few Jamaicans consumed, was much more dramatic and much more deadly. The coincidence of domestic neoliberal policies and structural adjustments with a burgeoning cocaine and crack industry in the 1980s proved a lethal combination for Jamaica.

Ironies abound. The drug trade is now faster, more sophisticated, more likely to use modern technology to avoid detection and to hide money. Yet it also relies more and more on human bodies, one of the most traditional forms of smuggling, to transport the product. Enforcement efforts, especially those driven by the United States and targeting supply sources, have actually resulted in increased drug traffic through the Caribbean. As radar and other forms of surveillance cover larger and larger swaths of the Caribbean, they miss the slower boats. While shippers, buyers, and dealers communicate by cell phone, government agencies frequently do not, and the drugs slip through.

4 | Wired on the islands

From the perspective of people living in the Caribbean, the transformation of telecommunications and information technologies was probably much more life-altering than the collapse of the Berlin Wall. It is by now commonplace to observe the ways in which Internet connectivity reshaped the lives of millions in the Americas. Whether people have access to computers and the Internet or not, it has affected everything around them: business practices, financial transactions, policing, marketing, and interpersonal relationships. The speed and volume of telecommunications have rendered the world more interconnected than ever imagined. When proponents of this new age begin to proclaim utopian fantasies about the ability of the Internet to promote both democratization and greater prosperity throughout most of the world, critics invoke the "digital divide." The enormous changes wrought by the information revolution have not and will not create a more equitable world, they argue, but will only exacerbate the inequalities that already exist. Those in the wired zone will benefit from access to information, goods, employment opportunities, and more efficient governance. Those outside will suffer and get left farther behind. In fact, like much industrial change the telecommunications revolution will take advantage of global inequalities to build greater prosperity for some on the backs of exploited labor. That the telecommunications revolution has affected lives is not in question, but how and to what extent the benefits are shared is.

Observers within the Caribbean have buttressed both utopian claims and troubled predictions with the specifics of local cases. The region has been most profoundly affected by three changes in telecommunications and information technologies: the explosive growth of telephone use with the introduction of cellular phones, the emergence of data processing as an important sector of local

Caribbean economies, and the role of the Internet in the development of an offshore gambling industry. The question that arises from these new practices is not so much one of exploitation, but rather the extent to which Caribbean people have taken advantage of new technologies to change or improve their lives. The jury is still out.

Cellular phones

In June 2003, the *Small Islands Voice* reported that high school principals and teachers in St Vincent and the Grenadines were complaining about cell phones. Too many of them were ringing in class or in the library, and thus distracting everyone. They also feared that the cost of maintaining cell phones would drive these teenagers to crime and violence. Already, a woman and her daughters had pummeled another woman for stealing their cell phone. These incidents hint at the significance of cellular phones in this part of the world. Because of the prior existence of land lines in most of North America, consumers often acquired cell phones as a secondary means of communication. In the Caribbean, however, the cell phone has entered a market with fewer land lines and in many cases has become the only phone service available. The digital divide is all too evident in the distribution of cell phones throughout the Caribbean. Jamaica experienced the most dramatic transition. Rates of cellular phone ownership leapt from 10 per cent in 1999 to nearly 65 per cent in 2004. These rates are higher than Argentina, the United States (60 per cent), or other Anglophone islands. Trinidad and Tobago, for instance, has ownership rates of 40 per cent, while Antigua and Barbudas are at 50 per cent. Haiti, on the other hand, has remained largely outside the cellular network, reaching only 10 per cent in 2004. Although rates of ownership have accelerated lately in Haiti, they are still the lowest in the Caribbean, aside from Cuba, where cellular phones are available only for rent by visitors. In the Dominican Republic, rates of ownership have grown from 10 per cent in 1999 to about 30 per cent in 2004. The wealthier French departments have higher rates, approximating Jamaican numbers. In Guadeloupe, where telephone service is subsidized, rates in 1999 were 12 per cent, the highest in the Caribbean. By 2004 they matched Jamaica at nearly 65 per cent.

Part of this story reflects recent challenges to the monopoly held by Cable and Wireless, a British telecommunications corporation operating in the Caribbean for 130 years, starting originally as the Eastern Telegraph Company. Without competitors, Cable and Wireless was able to control the telecommunications infrastructure, updating it only when they deemed it necessary. Deregulation allowed Jamaicans to open their markets to competitors, who were able to take advantage of pent-up demand for a cheaper, more widely available telephone service. In 2000 Jamaica granted a telecommunications license to Digicel, a company founded by the Irish businessman Denis O'Brien. O'Brien had spent $300 million creating a cellular phone network, with 680 stations across the island. Once he obtained his license, he began to sell telephones. Until then, very few Jamaicans owned cell phones. Within 100 days, O'Brien had persuaded 100,000 more to buy one. By 2005, in a population of 2.5 million, 1.7 million owned cellular telephones.

Cellular phone use has changed the daily lives of Jamaicans, particularly those in small rural towns. Access to a telephone line usually meant a visit to a "phone box," mostly located in public spaces. These afforded little privacy, especially if the normal long line of waiting callers had gathered. Making long-distance calls was expensive and cumbersome. Most people called their relatives and friends abroad collect and then waited for them to call back. Cellular phones have altered both local and distant relationships. People now have direct access to local emergency and medical services and much easier contact with friends and family. If those friends or family are abroad, as are so many Jamaicans, cellular phones have enabled divided families to talk much more frequently, senders of remittances can confirm receipt quickly, and lovers and spouses can share, at least vicariously, daily lives. As with other technologies, the benefits do not come unconditionally. Some Jamaicans lament the feelings of greater surveillance and deepened dependencies that are the downside of the ability to contact anyone, any time.

From Jamaica, Digicel expanded its operations to other anglophone islands. It captured 50 per cent of the St Vincent and St Lucia markets in just six weeks. Over four years, it spent $600 million to get licenses in Aruba, Barbados, Cayman Islands, Grenada, the Grenadines, Jamaica, St Lucia, and St Vincent. It has also expanded to Guyana, Trinidad and Tobago, Antigua, Bahamas, and Turks and Caicos, as well as the Dutch Caribbean and Haiti. The coverage reflects some of the inequalities so prevalent in the Caribbean. Within the islands, cellular phone service is much more accessible in the urban centers than in the rural areas, although the latter are not completely isolated. At the same time, the presence of a single company with such widespread coverage means that it is more possible, and less expensive, to make telephone calls between the islands, even between the anglophone, francophone, and Dutch islands, which traditionally have had very weak ties to one another.

With a competitor in the market, Cable and Wireless responded aggressively, and prices fell. But Digicel has diversified its tactics. It has worked to create a corporate image as participant and benefactor in people's lives. After Hurricane Ivan in 2004, it donated $3 million in aid to Grenada. It wins even more public notice by sponsoring the West Indies cricket team and contributing to numerous charitable organizations and festivals.

Internet

While the cellular phone revolution has owed much to forward-looking businessmen and the enthusiasm of customers, Internet connectivity has relied more on international and government agencies in the face of some hesitation by potential users. In the early 1990s dozens of conferences hailed the possibilities of the Caribbean as an information society. Some of their projects have come to fruition. Others have not.

Even the poorest states have embraced Information and Communications Technology (ICT). In 2001, the president of Guyana declared at the opening of Parliament: "modern communications technologies should be employed in our battle to break down cultural barriers, root out illiteracy and backwardness and expand the horizons of our people." Information technology could also be a source of foreign investment and jobs for struggling economies: "we must be prepared to compete globally for our share of the information age businesses and jobs ... Competition and enabling of the telecom business environment will bring IT investments to Guyana, which will create high-paying IT jobs." Wealthier islands had further plans for ICT. Some hoped for greater transparency and participation in government. Barbados created GOBINET, an information network that allows Barbadians to communicate directly with the government. Realizing IT's obvious pedagogical values, many pledged to put computers in schools and integrate them into curricula. In Grenada, the government welcomed new aids for law enforcement and envisioned a system that would digitize criminal and immigration data along with identity material such as fingerprints.

According to a study published in 2000 by Daniel Miller and Don Slater, Trinidadians have embraced the Internet fully. Arguing that Internet use on the islands ought to be understood as embedded in social contexts and practices rather than as an exotic imposition resulting from "globalization," they have examined use among ordinary Trinidadians in a number of mundane settings. Very quickly, Trinidadians have integrated the Internet into their lives. Although there are not that many private, individual accounts, these are shared widely among many generations, extending availability to older people who in other contexts have been left out of this transformation. Internet cafés and connected computers in libraries mean that those who are less well off can use the Internet. Perhaps more surprising, the authors claim that they do use it, recalling conversations about email and Internet providers during visits to homes without running water or electricity. Rather than giving rise to brand-new practices, Internet use has inserted itself into long-standing habits and practices. Trinidadians use email to enhance long-distance relationships and churches reach out to congregations through websites. Trinidadians have used the Internet to proclaim and reinforce their "Trini" identities, visiting the "Miss Universe" website, or creating chat groups of Trinidadians abroad. Rather than being an abstract space or one dominated by global media, it is a place that Trinidadians have filled and expanded into with specific cultural content. In that sense, the local and the global create one another.[1]

Similarly, but within completely different parameters, in Cuba Internet access reflects prevailing social and political practices. Yet outside observers and Cubans alike disagree on the meaning and consequences of Internet access. The United States facilitated

Cuba's getting online by exempting telecommunications from the new restrictions of the anti-Castro Cuban Democracy Act of 1992. It undoubtedly if naïvely believed that greater information flows and new modes of mobilization would accelerate Castro's fall. The Cuban government had other ideas. It saw the Internet as a medium for disseminating pro-government information and for building solidarity networks to support the Cuban regime. The government has thus asserted its control over Internet access. It has limited the number of available accounts and doles them out with a careful glance at an organization's perceived loyalty. NGOs with Internet access have learned that it is a privilege quickly rescinded at the first sign of unauthorized activity. At the same time, sites that specifically promote the regime and its aims enjoy free rein, often with positive results. The government created Infomed, a website run by the Ministry of Public Health, to enable healthcare providers to contact one another and to receive medical updates on a regular basis. Tourist sites have helped strengthen that sector, and sites promoting the biotech industry present an image of efficiency and competence to potential clients. A study conducted in 1999 claimed that Cuba had set up 25,500 accounts sending messages internationally. For those with access, there is no censorship of the Web. In theory, though, such access is rare. The study noted that only 2,000 computers in the country had direct access. Libraries do not provide computers with access to the Web, and the few Internet cafés that exist are meant for tourists.

Despite the official denial of Internet availability to the majority of Cubans, things look a little different on the ground. In a highly literate society that has always valued technological capacity, many people are adept at the computer. And in a society that has adopted black market practices as a way of life at many levels, it is only natural that such activity would extend to the Internet. Illegal access exists at the highest levels; government-run companies have downloaded programs and software that might not be available legally. In a study published in 2005, reporter John Coté tracked the emergence of creative schemes to obtain Internet access. One computer technician, trained at an exclusive science-oriented high school, had been hired by a construction company for the express purpose of hacking and finding ways to avoid software copyright restrictions. Later he did freelance work for a company that designed software and websites. Along the way he also became expert at pirating Internet accounts and then renting or selling them to interested Cubans. He is part of a complicated system of black market accounts that has given Internet access, often from home, to thousands of Cubans who might not otherwise have it. In addition, given the great pressure on limited resources, many of these accounts are shared by dozens of users. While this is probably an urban phenomenon, Internet use has become part of everyday life among students, academics, and other sectors. Although the Cuban government tried to crack down on unsanctioned Internet access in 2004, the campaign seems to have had little effect. At the same time, growing access to the Internet does not appear to have translated, yet, into an increasing threat to the Cuban regime. Rather the regime and its citizens have adjusted to one another's demands: the regime overlooks black market activities, while its citizens devise new ways to get online.[2]

In Cuba as in other parts of the Caribbean, debates centered not on whether but on how to embrace information and communications technologies. Although it may be too early to decide the success or failure of these programs, it is nonetheless possible to begin a preliminary accounting of them. The contrasts (and similarities) between the Trinidadian and Cuban instances of Internet adoption suggest the power of domestic and political arrangements to mold local practices. Technologies, even those most widely available and seemingly divorced from social life, function only in specific contexts.

Education

In response to high rates of unemployment among Caribbean youth, many of the island nations have sought to remedy or alleviate this problem through education and training in information technologies. Barbados, Jamaica, St Lucia, and Trinidad and Tobago all initiated programs aimed at young people. They involve updating the infrastructure and technological capacities of high schools and reforming curricula to incorporate computer literacy and training. Some have created institutions dedicated exclusively to fostering computer literacy, such as Trinidad and Tobago's College of Science, Technology and Applied Arts and its Youth Training and Employment Partnership Programme. Jamaica's University of Technology has a Technology Innovation Centre to support computer-literate youth who may have ideas about how to utilize their talents to generate income. This has produced many success stories of young entrepreneurs using the training and available resources to set up flourishing Internet companies. In some ways these islands are ideal environments for the expansion of information technologies with the hopes of creating more employment. The workforce is highly educated, has high expectations, and is eager for retraining. The extent to which these measures will assuage the Caribbean's unemployment woes has yet to be revealed.

In the meantime, more and more schoolchildren view the computer as part of their daily classroom routine. It is here that diversity and inequality appear most obvious. In the rainforest of Suriname, pupils in the small village of Powakka have participated in a project to extend computer literacy to Amerindians of the interior. Begun in 1995, the program aimed at using ICT to rectify some of the weaknesses in the Surinamese educational system, particularly the isolation and shortage of trained secondary school teachers. The new network system would not only teach children to use computers but also provide access to distance learning centers in the capital city, Paramaribo. The program has also improved and expanded teacher education and even trained government workers, particularly in agribusiness. By 2004 twenty-two "knowledge centers," many of them in existing classrooms, had been established. The computers offer a stark contrast to the schools themselves, which often lack basic amenities like running water and essential educational materials like books or paper. The trade-off that many countries seem to have accepted involves pouring revenues into newer resources at the expense of more traditional ones, such as books and paper, in the hopes that this will pay off in the end.

If critics worry about a digital divide that may leave the Caribbean excluded from the information highway, it may be more appropriate to worry about several divides, rather than just one. Attention needs to go not only to the disparities in Internet access and computer skill level between North America or Europe and the Caribbean, but also to inequalities within the Caribbean, from one island to the next. The high-tech Antigua and Barbuda International Institute of Technology intends to create a working population that is fully computer literate. It was set up in 2001 at a cost of $6.2 million in Antigua's free trade zone with the specific goal of training students for employment within the free trade zone itself. With room for 1,440, it contains twelve classrooms with twenty computers each, an additional lab with ninety computers, and student facilities including a cafeteria and bookstore. Courses cover HTML programming and word processing as well as accounting, banking and finance, and business administration.

Digital divides also exist within countries. Barbados has devoted significant amounts of money and attention to developing ICT programs. In addition to promoting e-commerce and running one of the more successful data processing industries in the Caribbean, the government has created EduTech 2000, a broadly conceived program for educational reform. Emphasis on computer literacy formed part of a major pedagogical transition from rote and passive learning to the interactive and collaborative classroom. The program has installed computers and software in both primary and secondary schools but mostly in wealthy, urban areas. Even on an island as small as Barbados differential access is evident: while the wealthy and well educated participate in EduTech, others cannot enjoy this benefit at all.

Barbadians themselves have recognized how access to computer technology could exacerbate social divisions and have sought to alleviate the disparities. In 2000 they established a parallel program, the Community Technology Programme, which had links to EduTech, but targeted communities too poor to afford computers and keyboard classes or obtain Internet access. By 2003, ten centers had opened with 1,147 people enrolled. The participants and instructors faced a number of problems, such as inconsistent connectivity and modest financial disorganization, but over a thousand people complete these courses each year, and future plans envision the establishment of at least ten new centers annually.

These endeavors also have their critics. The website of EduTech itself alludes to some of them: "This component of EduTech is the most well-known and controversial. Some say funds should be spent on recruiting teachers instead of buying technology, others say students are doing more on computers than just researching projects." But such criticism does not seem to have slowed ICT development projects. Nearly every island has adopted some form of ICT.

In the Hispanic Caribbean, two examples of community telecenters reflect this growing interest in new technological practices. The Centro Rural Alternativo in Limón de Ocóa, Dominican Republic, has affected the daily lives of community members in unexpected ways. Unable to get telephone service from the local telephone company, residents established, with the assistance of an international organization affiliated with Cornell University, an Internet connection instead. The effects rippled through the small town. Residents began to rely increasingly on email to communicate with one another. This development also changed intergenerational relations, as once alienated youth became actively involved in providing services and information to those not so comfortable or adept with the technology. Most impressively, they used the Internet to garner international support for housing and agriculture projects from the United Nations Development Programme and the InterAmerican Foundation. By 2001, they were planning eventually to build educational facilities and set up a distance learning program.

In Cuba, the Joven Club de Computación y Electrónica (Youth Computing and Electronics Club) has over its thirteen years of operation established 175 telecenters. Each of these has different affiliations with local governments or health and educational institutions, but all claim to address specific, local needs. For instance, in Amancio de las Tunas, the telecenter devised a program to help delinquent youth. In Viñales, a busy tourist spot, the centers train people to work in the tourist sector. In Cabaiguán, possible solutions for river pollution are the focus of its telecenters. Whether these and other programs are as effective as they appear and whether ICT is essential for their operations are questions that warrant further study. The giddy rhetoric of project reports sees unlimited possibilities for ICT in the service of the revolution. Disillusioned participants point out that, despite good intentions, many of these clubs do not function in the way envisioned. They still struggle to obtain working computers and problem-free connections to the Internet.

The process of introducing the Internet is still young, much as in the rest of the world. Already it has altered the way people work, study, shop, and communicate with one another. The Caribbean is a particularly good example of the ways local social and political circumstances shape the ways communications technologies will be adopted. In some ways, though it is one of the most obvious and dramatic manifestations of "globalization," it has changed basic structures the least. The Internet reflects inequalities, but it also facilitates social exchanges. And social relations direct the ways the Internet will be used, not the other way around.

Data processing

Casting about for new sources of revenue, some Caribbean nations saw in offshore data processing a way to take advantage both of relatively high literacy rates and relatively low wages. Information processing was a new and rapidly growing industry that thrived on the combination of computer technology and telecommunications. Since the storage, transmission, organization and display of data need not be tied to the same city or even country as a company's main site of operations, it could be outsourced, thus following a major corporate trend. Businesses could use differential wage rates to lower their costs. In the early to mid-1980s this was occurring in many parts of the world, and the Caribbean joined in. While the Dominican Republic, Trinidad and Tobago, Grenada, and St Kitts all set up data processing centers, Jamaica and Barbados were the most systematic. As early as 1986, both islands began creating a work environment that would appeal to companies looking to move their data processing offshore. They did so with varying degrees of success.

Jamaica and Barbados tried to attract foreign companies in slightly different ways. As part of its general program to bring in foreign investment, Jamaica established several free trade areas, or "export processing zones," which provide facilities and infrastructure and offer financial incentives to potential investors. These grew very rapidly at first, but most of their success came from the garment industry, which grossed $317 million in 1995. The Jamaican government sought to diversify these zones by turning to information processing. It built Jamaica Digiport International (JDI) in one of the free trade areas in Montego Bay. JDI offered an advanced telecommunications system, equipped for data transmission, international long distance, and 800 numbers. With this updated technological capacity in place and new tax incentives, the Jamaican government hoped to entice foreign investors.

Information processing companies did emerge, increasing from only two in 1983 to thirty-seven in 1990. But contrary to expectations, they were generally locally owned, and, ironically, located mostly outside of the free trade zones. Without either the tax incentives intended for foreign companies or access to more efficient telecommunications connections, they did not flourish, and the numbers began to dwindle in the early 1990s. Other factors also contributed to the demise of information processing in Jamaica. In part, the problem was the changing nature of the industry during this period. Initially, one of Jamaica's advantages was its proximity to the United States, since paper documentation had to be shipped to the island for conversion to a computerized format. Once data moved electronically, shipping was no longer necessary and physical proximity was no longer relevant. The field also became much more competitive, as countries as far away as the Philippines, India, and China could offer comparable services at even lower cost.

A further weakness in the industry's structure soon emerged. Since the locally based companies relied solely on US contracts, they were dangerously vulnerable to the vagaries of these companies. The volume and flow of work were inconsistent. While American firms may have benefited from the presence of competing firms, the firms themselves suffered as they saw contracts come and go, and often failed to maintain consistent markets for their services.

All this made for very difficult labor relations within both the locally run and the few foreign-owned firms. Irregular employment meant low salaries and tenuous job security. With little incentive to keep regular hours, data processors often worked only long enough to earn a basic salary. There were few staff benefits. Many firms did not provide childcare, or transportation to the work site, or even comfortable work spaces, adequate lighting, and ergonomic keyboards.

Low worker motivation was also due to inequalities in the workplace. In many of these firms, the majority of data processors were female, while management was largely male. Not only did workers understand the tough odds against promotion, they also felt belittled and demeaned while at work. Thus, high turnover rates, low worker motivation, and weak firm loyalty created a vicious circle: poor labor relations produced an image of an inefficient workforce, which discouraged potential investors or contractors, which perpetuated the inconsistent demand for labor.

Barbados has been more successful in attracting the foreign investors and large companies that can provide steadier work and higher wage levels. The island's venerable data processing industry began in 1968 with a company that input punch card data into mainframe computers for clients in the United States. It grew during the early 1980s with the establishment of Caribbean Data Services, a company that processed airline coupons for American Airlines. The spurt came in the 1990s, however, so that by 1996 forty-eight companies were operating in Barbados, all of them benefiting from such attractive incentives as tax rates of 2.5 per cent, no taxes on capital gains, dividends, interest or royalties, and reimbursements for wages paid during training sessions in the company's first year. In Barbados, foreign-owned firms employ 88.5 per cent of workers in the information processing sector. Thirty-six companies focus on data management, while the remaining twelve provide essential support services such as technical assistance, hardware, and training.

The government has also assisted both foreign and locally owned businesses. When the industry faced major closures as a result of corporate buyouts and downsizing, the government created InfoTech 2000, to supplement EduTech 2000 and feed people into the informatics sector, both as workers and as entrepreneurs. The program set the ambitious goal of training workers who could tackle more sophisticated data entry projects. They would thus help achieve the government's larger plan of finding a niche and gaining an advantage over competing islands by capturing the higher end of the industry.

Labor and gender

While many of these firms provide working conditions no better than those in Jamaica, others appear to have succeeded in addressing some of the most egregious problems. Hence the range of working conditions and labor relations in Barbados is much wider than that in Jamaica. The oldest firm, Caribbean Data Services, ranks near the top. Unique among its competitors, its general manager is a Barbadian woman who began as a data processor. According to a 1999 study, the company owed part of its success to the importance it placed on health and safety in the workplace. It boasts a full-time nurse, a physiotherapist and a Department of Occupational Safety and Health. It also offers employees educational sessions, regular exercise breaks, massage, and ultrasound treatment. Although this firm is not unionized, it reports high job satisfaction among workers, who meet monthly with management, and are encouraged to participate in the firm's decision-making processes.

As in Jamaica, women dominate the labor force in the informatics industry, in part because of foreign companies' positive, if stereotyped, view of female labor. For them, women are docile, hardworking, and more adept at monotonous tasks that require meticulous attention to detail. Traditional family structures contribute to women's appeal, for many companies assume young women to be dependent on their immediate or extended families, and so less in need of the kinds of salaries that men might demand as heads of households. In fact many female workers are single mothers raising children on their own or supporting other family members. They work for whatever wages are available in order to provide for their families.

The high proportion of female workers has significant implications for the workplace and labor relations. Anthropologist Carla Freeman has studied women on the new "global assembly line" in Barbados. She looks at women workers not only as producers but as consumers as well. To be sure, these women participate in a global division of labor in which their low salaries and demanding work contribute to the considerable profits of the corporations involved. It would be easy to view these women as exploited victims of globalization, and there is of course a measure of truth to that description. But Freeman draws a more complex picture as she looks inside the workplace and tries to assess the women's experiences on their terms. Many of the women derive a certain amount of status from their jobs. Access to an income in itself allows women to assert an independence they might not otherwise be able to claim. Even if they earn less money than workers in other sectors, their working environment, with its air-conditioning, comfortable office furniture, and access to computer technology, sets them apart from other female workers, who toil in domestic service, grow and sell foodstuffs, or labor in a factory.

Furthermore, they derive satisfaction from the ways they choose to dress for their job. The women use their salaries for basic living expenses but they also spend much of their earnings on particular kinds of clothes. They dress up for the office in suits, dresses, high heels, and stockings. Although they do not meet with the public and see only one another at work, their appearance has become an important part of the job. Freeman argues that their situation is "alternately burdensome and pleasurable" as they adjust their lives to the pressures of data processing and craft feminine, professional selves with clothes and accessories they deem essential. Thus dressing well becomes an important part of their lives, and weekends are spent designing and making clothes, which they often sell or give to their colleagues. In public, office attire distinguishes them from other workers. Friends, strangers, boyfriends, and husbands note the way they dress as they walk to work or wait for public transit. They arouse both admiration and resentment. Freeman argues that, like many societies, Barbadians take appearances seriously. In effect, these women are developing new class statuses for themselves. The consumption of certain kinds of clothing leads to the production of new class identities.[3]

They also participate in a global economy of fashion, as they use their bonuses and vacations to make periodic trips to the United States, usually Miami or New York, to purchase numerous items of clothing to bring back home to wear, sell or give to friends, family, and peers. As Freeman observes, the production of Barbadian women's identities as "working girls" but not working-class girls requires the consumption of goods produced in another part of the global assembly line. She has named these women who have incorporated fashion into their transnational quest for social status "higglers," a term originally used to refer to Jamaican market women. The ways they take advantage of easier travel, mass-produced, affordable clothing, and their peers' awareness of global fashion demonstrates that globalization occurs on the ground among working people, not just in corporate boardrooms. The point, Freeman insists, with an emphasis on the role of agency, is not that these women are responding to globalization, but rather that they are creating it.[4]

Offshore money

It began in 1936, when British and Canadian firms set up operations in the Bahamas to protect the investments of some of their wealthier clients. Since then, offshore banking has grown into a multimillion-dollar enterprise with offices throughout the Caribbean. Most established are those in Antigua, the British Virgin Islands, and the Cayman Islands. Recent developments in telecommunications and computer technology have made banking so fast and easy that more islands, such as St Lucia and St Kitts, have begun to organize their own offshore agencies. Clients have placed their money in a broad range of financial institutions, including international business corporations (IBCs), offshore corporations, commercial banks, insurance companies, mutual funds, and gaming companies to avoid paying taxes in their home countries. These institutions are also ideal for money laundering.

Offshore banking operations have to negotiate between an appeal based precisely on their remote location and notions of backwardness so often part of the islands' reputations. Chambers of commerce, especially in the English-speaking Caribbean, work hard to remind potential customers of "long-standing legal traditions" and "highly educated English-speaking personnel." But they also remind clients of the unique experience of achieving important financial goals while basking in the sun or playing a few rounds of seaside golf. This is a winning combination, as evidenced by the many entrepreneurs, crooks, and heads of state who siphon funds to Caribbean locales. In a notorious example, the Enron scandal of

2001 revealed that company's creation of 700 partner companies registered in the Cayman Islands to avoid paying taxes.

The islands have benefited in numerous ways from these tax evasion and money laundering schemes. Not only do offshore institutions employ locals, they require a support infrastructure that ranges from hotels and restaurants to updated telecommunications and transportation systems. While the offshore banking industry may not be a major sector of the economy in all the islands, it does contribute significantly to some. In Antigua and Barbuda, the industry employs 8 per cent of the labor force; in the British Virgin Islands, 15 per cent of the labor force works in this sector. Its state fees cover 7 per cent of government revenue in Antigua and Barbuda, 4.5 per cent in Grenada, and a staggering 55 per cent in the British Virgin Islands. At the same time, but especially recently, the island nations have had to deal with increased scrutiny and surveillance, as well as threats to their sovereignty.

In the late 1990s concerns arising from serious financial crises stimulated efforts to monitor and control offshore banking operations more rigorously. The Financial Action Task Force, an intergovernmental organization established by the G-7, after investigating offshore financial practices, issued recommendations to make these more transparent and, in its eyes, legitimate. It urged *inter alia* international cooperation, more exchange of information about clients, and the closer supervision and regulation of transactions. In 2000 it issued a report that assigned some nations "cooperative" or "non-cooperative" status. To be non-cooperative meant failing to adopt some of those practices intended to assist in the identification and prosecution of money launderers. Fifteen of twenty-six countries were deemed non-cooperative. Some did reform their practices to conform to the recommendations, but others did not. They resented the increase in surveillance and publicity which, they argued, was driving off potential clients. For some observers, this policy is another instance of financial imperialism, as they point out the asymmetry of approach: why is tax evasion (or the flow of money from wealthier nations to poorer ones) perceived to be a problem, while capital flight (the flow of money from poorer nations to wealthier ones) is not?

Gambling

It does not take a very long Google search to arrive at an online casino. A few more clicks ensure that the casino is based somewhere in the Caribbean. Once the site comes up, a mellifluous welcome and a continuous steel-drum audio loop confirm its origins. The site is slick and enticing, even to someone who has never gambled before, online or off. You can play roulette, blackjack, poker, or slots for free. The voice talks you through the game. It is not difficult to play for money, until you try to pay. You discover your US credit cards will not work, and you have become part of an unfolding dispute that has embroiled the WTO, Antigua and Barbuda, and the United States, where 90 per cent of online gamblers reside, in arguments about free trade, morality, technology, and national sovereignty.

Of all the indicators of a telecommunications revolution in the Caribbean, online gambling has experienced the most spectacular growth. After their 1995 debut, the number of websites devoted to online gaming, including sports betting, online casinos and lotteries, rose from sixty in 1997 to 260 by 1999. Some reports claim that there were between 600 and 700 sites in 2000. Although revenue estimates vary, they are all staggering. In 1999 online sites drew in $600 million. While early predictions of earnings of $100 billion by 2006 seem highly inflated, recent, cautious estimates place revenues at $10 billion for 2000. Though frustratingly inconsistent, the wildly fluctuating numbers point to the profitable but elusive nature of this enterprise. Like offshore banking, online gaming has brought employment and income to struggling Caribbean nations. Antigua and Barbuda, with one of the more developed online gaming industries, has reported earnings of up to $20 million per year.

But gambling in cyberspace has raised a tangle of legal issues. National regulations and laws on gambling run the gamut from completely legal and state-sponsored to expressly forbidden. Most Caribbean nations now regulate their legal gambling operations, online and off. In Antigua, which boasts the most websites in the Caribbean, no regulatory mechanisms existed until the mid-1990s. The "Standard Conditions for Licensing of Virtual Casino Wagering and Sports Book Wagering in the Antigua and Barbuda Free Trade and Processing Zone" of 1997 empowered the state's free trade commission to licence and regulate sites. The new code prohibited the transfer of licenses, non-payment of commitments to players, and the dissemination of false promotional statements. To combat fraud, annual fees were set at $100,000 for a casino and $75,000 for sports betting. Antigua has begun to conduct background checks which, it claims, have already eliminated hundreds of applicants. In Dominica, the government controls and runs much of online gaming. Individuals may obtain casino licenses, but they have to agree to employ a certain number of Dominicans in their enterprises, and pay back a certain amount of the revenue to the state. In return, licensees have access to updated telecommunications systems and greater flexibility with work permits and the importation of equipment.

Tiny Antigua now lies at the center of a storm swirling around online gaming that has intensified a maelstrom about free trade, national sovereignty, and international law. Though the winds do not seem to have dispelled the murkiness of online gaming, this is an intriguing story of the WTO defending a small poor country against the demands of the United States. In this instance, globalization seems to have both overridden and reinforced national borders.

In the United States, gambling is legal in many states and Indian reservations, but placing or receiving bets across state or national lines remains a point of contention in the courts. In 1998, federal prosecutors indicted Jay Cohen and Steven Schillinger, the American owners of an online sports betting operation known as the World Sports Exchange and located in Antigua. Eventually a total of twenty-one owners and employees of Internet gambling companies were indicted, on the grounds that they had violated the Wire Communications Act. This was an unprecedented use of an act that dated back to 1961. True, it prohibited sports betting operations from receiving wagers that were wired across state or national boundaries, but it had not been revised to take into account Internet and online gaming. Of the twenty-one indicted owners, operators, and managers of offshore betting operations in Costa Rica, Curaçao, the Dominican Republic, and Antigua, eleven pleaded guilty and six fled to avoid prosecution. Only Jay Cohen's case went to trial. In 2000 a US district court in Manhattan found him guilty of violating the federal wire act and sentenced him to twenty-one months in prison.

This was enough, apparently, to encourage US lawmakers to write further legislation to prohibit, or at least limit, online gaming. Initial attempts, while the case was still ongoing, included a proposed Internet Gambling Prohibition Act which would have outlawed the placing and receiving of bets. It passed the Senate 90–10, but died on the House floor. Critics stressed the impracticability of enforcement. Undeterred, Congress tried another approach. In 2001 the House subcommittee on crime entertained two proposals, the "Unlawful Internet Gambling Funding Prohibition Act" and the "Combating Illegal Gambling Reform and Modernization Act." After several years Congress passed a bill that barred credit card companies, banks, and other financial institutions from transferring money to online gaming operations. Unlikely coalitions had formed to support and oppose restrictions on online gaming. Championing the prohibitions was an alliance of Christian evangelist groups opposed to gambling on moral grounds and sports associations, including Major League baseball and horse-track operators, along with convenience store and liquor store owners, all of whom feared competition from online gambling operations. Against restrictions were Republican governors and the operators of online gambling sites, including owners of Internet casino operations in the Caribbean.

Antigua and Barbuda claimed that this act adversely affected their online gaming industry. The number of its Internet betting and gaming companies had fallen from 100 in 2002 to only thirty-six in 2004, costing the island nation tens of millions of dollars in revenues and hundreds of jobs. At this point Antigua turned to the WTO. It charged that the prohibition of Internet gaming contradicted free trade agreements that the USA had signed with Antigua. In 2004, the WTO decided in favour of Antigua and Barbuda, declaring that "certain US laws run counter to that country's commitments to Antigua and Barbuda under the WTO's General Agreement on Trade Services." While the USA invoked the demons of terrorism, money laundering and gambling addiction in its defense, Antigua and Barbuda claimed that one of the principal motives for the law was to eliminate competition with US-run gaming operations.

When the US government appealed the decision, the rhetoric of the conflict escalated. Antiguan prime minister Baldwin Spenser met with a US congressional delegation and asked the USA to withdraw its appeal. He pleaded the innocent victim: "to this island of under 70,000 people, with an economy in bad shape, the US actions in the Internet gaming issue appear to go to a level of shock and awe that a friendly small nation has done nothing to deserve." He also employed the language of free trade benefits that has become so irrefutable: "we believe that as a small nation fighting very hard to find certain niches so that we can boost our economy and find employment for our people, the offshore financial sector, Internet gaming and other related activities are important for our economy, and the US would appear to be opposed to this. This is against the WTO's idea of international trade and opening up the region for cross-border business activities."[5] In February 2005, CARICOM, the Caribbean economic organization, sided with Antigua and Barbuda in the dispute. Two months later, the WTO decided on the USA's appeal in such a way that both sides can claim victory. On one hand, the appeals panel agreed that the United States had made a strong case for the relevance of the 1961 Wire Communications Act and its prohibitions on interstate gambling in order to "protect public safety and morals." On the other hand, it also ruled that the United States did not have clear jurisdiction in its attempts to regulate foreign gambling operations. United States representatives read the judgment to say: "WTO members are entitled to maintain restrictions on Internet gambling ... as long as the US clarifies certain Internet gambling restrictions, it will be in compliance with WTO rules." Antigua denied this interpretation; it insisted: "the ruling would force the US to negotiate a compromise." As of this writing, the dispute continues. In November 2006, the WTO's Dispute Settlement Body began hearings at Antigua's behest. The island nation challenged the United States' claim that it was complying with WTO rules. In effect, Antigua is still accusing US limitations on online gambling of violating free trade agreements.[6]

This case may last for a long time, but in the meantime online gaming companies in Antigua and other Caribbean nations have devised ways to circumvent US prohibitions on credit card payments to gaming websites. The websites offer an array of possible forms of payment, each technically legal. Although PayPal has dropped its services to online gaming companies, similar companies based else-where have stepped in. Gamblers can use NETeller or E-CashWorld, companies based outside the United States, in the same way as they would have used PayPal. Another option is the bank debit card, since banks have no way of monitoring how the cards are used. Many Caribbean gambling companies have also sought players outside the United States, so a substantial portion of their business now comes from Europe and Asia. In a peculiar twist, tiny islands have found ways to increase the flow of money across borders, while the United States cries foul.

Conclusion

Telecommunications and computer technologies have changed the lives of Caribbean people, but they have not proven to be the homogenizing eliminators of local cultures that some imagined. Caribbeans have used these resources as they use other resources, with wariness, creativity, and a wide range of outcomes. Across the region, people can speak to one another more easily and commu-nicate with friends and relatives abroad. They have adopted new ways to work and found that those in turn facilitate shifts in social statuses. While in some ways they have been drawn into the orbit of the United States, they have worked to exercise some control over that relationship. Indeed far from homogenizing, greater access to technologies has in some ways sharpened social and economic divisions among Caribbeans, bringing into relief the inequalities and fragmentation so characteristic of the region. In its multiple dimensions the way Caribbeans have engaged with communica-tions technologies underscores the fact that, for them, globalization happens at home.

Conclusion: on history

Caribbean nations negotiated the challenges of recent history within parameters set by structural continuities and historical legacies. Economic hardship, either directly imposed as a result of the fall of the Soviet Union or ushered in as economies were brought into line with neoliberal principles that advocated decreased social spending, posed one of the most significant obstacles. While this eliminated many options for governments and their citizens, it did not necessarily create uniformity within the region. To the contrary, the Caribbean remains politically and socially diverse, both within and among the islands.

Working within constraints to create new options, the island nations drew on the very mobilities that shaped their earlier histories and reinvented their place in the world. Haitians abroad used their transnational condition to participate in a transition from dictatorship to democracy. When aid was withheld because of perceptions of "instability," some were able to take advantage of differential income levels between the United States and Haiti to assist those at home. As Cuba sought and obtained foreign investment it reinvented the revolution, re-emphasizing nationalism and downplaying anti-capitalism. It benefited as well from the very recent backlash against the neoliberal hegemonies among Latin American states. When the imposition of austerity measures significantly weakened the social safety net, some Jamaicans found in the cocaine trade a way to attenuate marginalization. At the same time, they began to challenge the global regime criminalizing marijuana which didn't make sense in a domestic context. All over the Caribbean global communications technologies were used to meet local needs, whether those were maintaining ties with friends and relatives, luring foreign investors, or creating opportunities for education and employment.

But this is not a heroic story or a romantic tale of happy endings. Each of these contributions to the globalized world has come with a cost. Social inequality has increased throughout the Caribbean. Old rifts between the wealthy and the poor have acquired new faultlines, as divisions emerged between those who can and cannot travel, or between those with access to foreign resources and technologies and those who are not so fortunate. The incapacitation of states and flows of weapons exacerbated the violence that plagued Haiti and Jamaica. In the face of diminishing opportunities at home, migration and concomitant social dislocation remain the central aspect of many people's lives. In all these changes the networks of commodities and information have accelerated and intensified. Some observers interpret this as evidence of the region's continuing structural dependency and invest it with negative connotations. Others see it as the only way for the Caribbean to carry on in a rapidly changing world.

This might be the place to speculate on future developments, but thankfully that is not a historian's task. Instead I close this book with an invocation of Caribbean discussions about the role of history and historical memory. Even as they found themselves catapulted into the future, inhabitants of the Caribbean took time to reflect on the past. Despite the stock representations of the Caribbean as a place out of time, people who reside there have thought a great deal about how best to understand the processes and transformations the region has undergone over time. As with the lighthouse controversy in the Dominican Republic, anniversaries provided the opportunities to reopen discussions about historical memory. Recently, several of these occasions have commemorated slavery and its abolition. Along with all the other questions and obstacles they have encountered over the last twenty years, Caribbeans have immersed themselves in debates over the meaning and memory of slavery and its legacies.

In the French *départements* of Guadeloupe and Martinique, a battle over public history that began with the 1998 celebrations of the 150th anniversary of the abolition of slavery in 1848 has intensified ever since. As Catherine Reinhardt has observed in her book *Claims to Memory: Beyond Slavery and Emancipation in the French Caribbean*, many reconstructed monuments and visitor sites offer a memory of the colonial era that ignores slavery. In Habitation La Grivelière, a restored plantation in Guadeloupe, the big house has been carefully and beautifully rebuilt, while the slave quarters remain in ruins. In Guadeloupe's Musée du Rhum, informative labels and notes trace the entire trajectory of sugar cane, from harvest to processing to rum-making, without mentioning slavery or the slaves themselves. These and many similar memorials and monuments recall a sterile colonial past, emptied of the coercive labor of Africans and of their cultural inventions in music, religion, and healing.[1]

But the approach of 1998 unleashed the question of how slavery should be remembered and commemorated. The ceremonies and events planned for both France and the Caribbean were originally envisioned by officials as celebrations of the emancipation decree itself and its principal French proponent, Victor Schoelcher. They seemed to have forgotten both the earlier abolition edict of 1794 during the French and Haitian revolutions and slavery's return ten years later under Napoleon. Hence, instead of fixing a memory as may have been intended, the projected commemoration set off a series of debates on the islands about what precisely ought to be remembered. Many islanders protested that the official celebrations as organized by the French government would allow for the complete omission of any memory of slavery. Was there a place to remember slavery and the slave trade itself? Was there a place to remember the many acts of resistance and rebellion that may have accelerated the declaration of emancipation? Was there a place to remember the range of motivations that lay behind the apparently humanitarian act of freeing slaves?

The concrete results of this debate now dot the island. In fact, as historian Laurent Dubois has pointed out, "on both the official and unofficial levels, the celebration of 1848 was transformed on a number of levels into a celebration of the 1790s." The statues that were built memorialized the slaves Louis Delgrès, who fought the French invasion of Guadeloupe in 1802, and Ignace and Solitude, who, like Delgrès, struggled against the French army and died in those struggles. Residents of the island have begun to set up museums and memorials that depict slaves as they would like them remembered: as strong resisters and survivors, maroons who fled and refused slavery, women who instigated revolts, or people who worked and died with dignity.[2]

Such a dedicated response to the problem of commemoration apparently kept the debate, which continued until very recently, alive. In May 2001, the French passed a law that denoted slavery and the slave trade as crimes against humanity. Three years later, in January 2004, the government created a committee for the memory of slavery. Its recommendations the following year included the adoption of 10 May as the day of national commemoration for the abolition of slavery, greater incorporation of lessons on slavery and the slave trade in school curricula, and the establishment of research centers for the study of slavery and the slave trade. President Jacques Chirac accepted these recommendations in January 2006 and presumably worked to implement them.

Some of these adjustments may be better as beginnings rather than endings. As Haitian anthropologist Michel-Rolph Trouillot pointed out even before these events, how precisely to remember slavery requires careful consideration. Trouillot rightly argued for the integration of the memory of the Haitian revolution into the chronologies of world history, European history, and especially Caribbean history. As he observed, the Haitian revolution was long absent from such accounts. He cited the omission of the Haitian anti-colonial and abolitionist struggles from such texts as the Penguin *Dictionary of Modern History* or Eric Hobsbawm's *The Age of Revolutions: 1789–1843*. Backed by these somewhat astonishing examples, he made an eloquent case for locating the origins of this forgetting in the unthinkability of the event itself at the time it occurred and in the legacies of that unthinkability in mainstream histories.

At the same time, he argued that even existing accounts of the Haitian revolution in both Haiti and North America need to be probed for the ways they narrate the events. Some depict the revolution as a noble struggle of dedicated and single-minded slaves and former slaves united to overthrow their colonial masters. This is the "heroic romantic" version. On the other hand, there is what Trouillot labels the banalization of the revolution, found in histories so focused on the details of battles and diplomacy that they lack any overarching interpretive thrust. The actors in this version are not noble, nor do they have a particular vision; they are mostly creatures of circumstance and contingency.[3] For him these differences over the memory of slavery involve conflicting perspectives on human epistemologies and ontologies. These understandings inform different strands of historical memory and historiography. On one hand, narratives that depend on heroic slaves suggest a false sense of coherence and unity among what was in reality a fractious collection of African-born or Haitian-born slaves and former slaves with a number of competing agendas. On the other hand, narratives that rely on a mass of detail and invoke historical contingency may deflect questions about the politics of the revolution and thus fail to challenge an inadequate status quo.

Other Caribbean writers take up where Trouillot leaves off. Jamaica Kincaid notes a similar tendency in the remembrance of the past on her native island of Antigua. But she moves in a different direction. Where Trouillot focuses on the rewriting of the revolution as a way to rethink a legacy of unsatisfying histories, Kincaid suggests that dwelling on slave societies is in itself an obstacle. Antiguans, she says, are "obsessed with slavery"; the slavery that obsessed them, however, is a thin version, shaped by all kinds of forgetfulness. In their accounts, slavery was a harsh and cruel pageant, peopled by slaves who were "noble and exalted" and masters who were "rubbish." And suddenly it was over; emancipation had come. Antiguans remember emancipation, she claims, as if it were the recent past. It is not just that they remember slavery and its abolition to the exclusion of the histories of the latter part of the nineteenth and the twentieth centuries. The problem, for Kincaid, is that the "obsession with slavery" has sustained the life of certain categories, so that people are thought of as either "noble" or "rubbish." In the current era of decolonization this will not do. Since the descendants of slaves have now come to occupy positions of power, a one-dimensional moral framework allows for blindness towards the widespread corruption and environmental degradation that characterize present-day Antigua. Once Antiguans shed those categories and see human beings rather than "slaves" or "masters," they will be better equipped to understand their pasts, to see the present more clearly, and to struggle for a more just and equitable future. What this entails, in part, is paying attention to what occurred after emancipation.[4] To leave historical memory at the moment of abolition only reinforces the notion of the Caribbean as an incomplete project, as a people still in its infancy, a series of islands on the brink of modernity. The legacies of slavery demand attention, but so too do the legacies of all that came after, of post-emancipation, struggles for racial and economic justice, successful and failed projects of modernization, processes of decolonization and neocolonialism, and cultural and political polarizations.

Many Caribbean film-makers and novelists have made similar suggestions in their work. Euzhan Palcy's film *Sugar Cane Alley* begins rather than ends with emancipation. Set in 1930s Martinique, the film follows the young boy José as he confronts racism and poverty but also finds beauty, joy, and hope. His village may be poor and remote, but it is still a richly human place that provides community and friendship. José, however, receives a scholarship to study in the city, and he encounters at school the ongoing presence of colonizers in the classroom, in the textbooks, in the rigid rules of grammar and composition. Yet like the world around him, José incorporates all these experiences, and emerges neither derivative nor somehow colonized, but whole and original.

Adopting a very different tone, the brilliant Cuban film-maker Tomás Gutierrez Alea has chronicled the Cuban revolution and in the process reflects on the role of memory and the writing of history. *Death of a Bureaucrat*, in which the family of a deceased worker struggles with the Kafkaesque bureaucracy that refuses to issue a death certificate until it sees his identity card, which, because of his fame as an outstanding worker, was buried with him, both gently mocks the revolution and questions the legitimacy of history-making. No one entity can lay claim to truth: neither the dead man's family, who have a corpse as evidence, nor a labyrinthine state with its various methods of recording and storing the documents that purport to tell the truth. In the end the pursuit of history appears a futile endeavor; what matters is the location of the corpse in the present. Beyond this commentary on historical truth or its absence, a large proportion of Gutierrez Alea's output centers on recent history. With the exception of the masterful *The Last Supper*, set in post-Haitian revolution Cuba, most of his films tellingly observe the vagaries and absurdities of life in the Cuban revolution. His subject, insistently so, is the present. But it is a present that undermines most assumptions, narratives, and categories professed by the revolution. Observing the present becomes a way to question the fixity of the past.

The 2007 commemorations of the 200th anniversary of the British abolition of the slave trade provided residents of the anglophone islands and their counterparts in Britain with an opportunity to continue the dialogues about slavery and historical memory. At issue was not so much whether slavery would be remembered, but how, and whether it is ever possible to make amends for past injustices. As they began to form committees and plan ceremonies, some intellectuals and civic leaders proposed a series of actions through which they thought the British government might remedy the wrongs of the slave trade. These raised a series of questions about how to understand the past in relation to the present: was it a debt owed that needed to be paid off? Was it part of a past that needed at the very least to be publicly displayed and accepted as an episode in an unfolding pageant? Was it a legacy that had real consequences in terms of ongoing social inequality that ought to be remedied by offering more by way of opportunity?

Prime Minister Tony Blair set the tone by publishing an article in November 2006 in which he expressed sorrow and regret over Britain's role in the slave trade. He reiterated this publicly in a ceremony that took place several months later in Elmina Castle in Ghana and was videocast to the United Kingdom and locations in the former British empire. In Jamaica, critics immediately deemed Blair's stance inadequate. Some echoed the Archbishop of York's call for a full apology, from which Blair had pointedly refrained. Others were more concerned to move beyond debates over apologies towards more tangible outcomes.

Some Jamaicans sought widespread symbolic recognition. Through CARICOM, they successfully proposed that the United Nations adopt a resolution designating 25 March 2007 as a day of commemoration of the abolition of the slave trade. Others envisioned a more local impact. Former prime minister Edward Seaga offered a proposal centered on physical sites of commemoration.

Noting the building boom that preceded the opening of the cricket World Cup in the West Indies in the spring of 2007, he pointed out that no plans existed to build a museum to commemorate slavery or the slave trade in Jamaica. Although the Institute of Jamaica, which houses the National Library and the National Gallery, contained what he described as a "treasure trove of artefacts of cultural heritage, books, natural history, archaeology, biodiversity and ethnic diversity," it was located in a marginal neighborhood and so received very few visitors. Seaga called for the building of a national museum that would place Jamaica's "rich cultural panorama" on display, for residents and visitors alike.[5]

Rex Nettleford, vice-chancellor emeritus at the University of the West Indies and a distinguished historian, was neither interested in wresting apologies nor in a mood to celebrate Jamaican culture. Instead he proposed an action he thought would more immediately redress continuing injustices. The best way for Great Britain to demonstrate its contrition would be through creating a series of scholarships and fellowships to the University of the West Indies, which, as Nettleford pointed out, consistently served as an "escape route for a great many out of the endemic poverty which has plagued the islands for many years." Nettleford observed that while plantation owners had received compensation, the slaves hadn't. As well, the end of the slave trade did not mean the end of slavery, which continued for decades afterwards. Opportunities to obtain an education would be, in his view, a fitting way to remember not just the abolition of the slave trade but the reality of marginalization.[6]

As chair of the Jamaican National Bicentenary Committee, historian Verene Shepherd faced a formidable task. Under her direction the committee planned a year's worth of events and activities, with a focus on slaves and their descendants rather than on the British men who campaigned against the trade. In the end those plans reveal a sensibility that resonates with the injunctions of Trouillot and Kincaid, as they both remember slavery but also look beyond its demise. Rather than focus on a single moment in time, planned celebrations would include tributes to many prominent descendants of slaves who lived throughout the nineteenth and twentieth centuries, such as black activist Marcus Garvey and singer Bob Marley. In addition, a conference would explore the lives of maroons, or runaway slaves, and a public lecture preceding the opening of the cricket World Cup would point out the roles of descendants of slaves in the early development of cricket. The plans also included the unveiling of a series of monuments, which, like those in Guadeloupe, would be placed at sites around the island where slaves had disembarked. In this context, monuments dedicated to slaves upon their arrival make a somewhat poetic contribution to the debates over history and memory. In a very concrete fashion they mark the land and create a site of public history. As historians and intellectuals struggle to find ways to incorporate the past into the present, or vice versa, these monuments very literally unify the two. As a structure that invokes the past rests on land that has endured and witnessed historical transformations, a monument may embody the struggle to find usable pasts more succinctly and clearly than other efforts.

In his 1992 Nobel Lecture, St Lucian poet Derek Walcott worries about history. Seeming to echo Nietzsche's caution not to allow "the past to be the gravedigger of the present," he warns that "we make too much of that long groan which underlines the past." Walcott begins by describing a play performed in Felicity, Trinidad, as part of a Hindu festival. After chastising himself for mocking its lack of authenticity, he realizes it is his own expectation of authenticity which is the problem. We miss the point, he argues, if what we expect is a perfect reconstruction of things past. Perhaps it would prove more satisfying to celebrate a newly invented present that uses fragments of the past to create new cultural forms, as do the performers and their audience. Walcott devotes most of his Nobel Lecture to reflecting on how to reconcile pasts and presents without losing sight of either.

He writes about the historiography of the Caribbean as one of contempt in many guises. Composed mostly by outsiders who never settled and hence, according to him, could not "see" the place, these histories view the Caribbean as unfinished or always in the making. The fault was largely history's: "There was this conviction in Froude that since History is based on achievement, and since the history of the Antilles was so genetically corrupt, so depressing in its cycles

New York Times, 3 April 1989; "Gorbachev signs treaty with Cuba", *New York Times*, 5 April 1989.

3 Jon Lee Anderson, "Castro's last battle: can the revolution outlive its leader?", *New Yorker*, 31 July 2006.

4 Louis A. Pérez Jr, *Cuba and the United States: Ties of Singular Intimacy* (Athens: University of Georgia Press, 1990); Louis A. Pérez Jr, *On Becoming Cuban: Identity, Nationality, and Culture* (Chapel Hill: University of North Carolina Press, 1999).

5 Peter Sanford, "Sherritt International and Canadian–Cuban economic relations, 1989–1996" (University of British Columbia: 2006, Unpublished ms.).

6 Julie Feinsilver, *Healing the Masses: Cuban Health Politics at Home and Abroad* (Berkeley: University of California Press, 1993).

7 Pan American Health Organization, *Health in the Americas*, vol. 2, 2002.

8 Fidel Castro, "Speech to the students graduating from the Havana Higher Institute of Medical Sciences: Karl Marx Theater, 1999", <www.cuba.cu/gobierno/discursos/1999/ing/f090899i.html>. Accessed 6 December 2006.

9 "Evo Morales marca distancia con George Bush y se acerca a Castro", *La Razón*, 30 December 2005.

10 "Castro cree que con Morales el mapa político regional cambió", *La Razón*, 31 December 2005; "Clausuraron la cumbre alternativa en Viena Morales y Hugo Chávez", *Correo del Sur*, 14 May 2006.

11 Alejandro Portes and Alex Stepick, *City on the Edge: The Transformation of Miami* (Berkeley: University of California Press, 1993).

3 The traffic

1 Barry Chevannes, "Ganja and the road to decriminalization in Jamaica", in Ross Coomber and Nigel South (eds), *Drug Use and Cultural Contexts 'beyond the West': Tradition, Change and Post-Colonialism* (Free Association Books, 2004), p. 179.

2 Paul Gootenberg (ed.), *Cocaine: Global Histories* (New York: Routledge, 1999).

3 Laurie Gunst, *Born Fi' Dead: A Journey through the Jamaican Posse Underworld* (New York: Holt, 1995), pp. xx–xxi.

4 Marlyn Jones, "Policy paradox: implications of the US drug control policy for Jamaica", *Annals of the American Academy of Political and Social Sciences*, 582 (2002): 117–33.

5 Geoff Small, *Ruthless: The Global Rise of the Yardies* (London: Warner, 1995), p. 449.

6 Amanda Sives, "From politician to drug don: clientelism in downtown Kingston, Jamaica", *Latin American Perspectives*, 29(5): 66–89.

7 Small, *Ruthless*, p. 230.

of massacres, slavery, and indenture, a culture was inconceivable and nothing could ever be created in those ramshackle ports, those monotonously feudal sugar estates." These outsiders described what they thought they saw, but they were looking through glasses colored by a bleak historical memory. They missed the point; even their romanticized nineteenth-century portraits expressed contempt through egotistic misunderstanding, for they had more to do with the authors' concerns for disappearing landscapes in Europe than they did with the light and sea of the Caribbean: "A century looked at a landscape furious with vegetation in the wrong light and with the wrong eye."

The way to correct histories like these, he argues, is through writing and remembering that contains within it all the layers of the distant and recent past, as well as of the ongoing present. He invokes the image of a shattered vase that has been put back together as a metaphor for poetry and its relationship to the past. The unbroken vase travels through time and space, embedded in certain histories. Its reconstitution is an act of love and care, an awareness, which may not have been there before, of the fragments and their meaning. The glue, he continues, is the care with which the poet or artist can take shards of the past, fragments created in pain and destruction, and rework them into something beautiful that neither forgets nor remembers perfectly. Poetry, like the daily sunrise that is central to Walcott's rituals of writing, can see a beautiful present that contains but is not overwhelmed by difficult pasts:

> It is not that History is obliterated by this sunrise. It is there in Antillean geography, in the vegetation itself. The sea sighs with the drowned from the Middle Passage, the butchery of its aborigines, Carib and Aruac and Taino, bleeds in the scarlet of the immortelle, and even the actions of surf on sand cannot erase the African memory, or the lances of cane as a green prison where indentured Asians, the ancestors of Felicity, are still serving time.

The challenge as he sees it is to let the landscape write itself, rather than being written. In that sense the monuments to arriving slaves in both Guadeloupe and Jamaica may serve as examples. By calling for writing that, like the monuments, is firmly rooted in place, taking in the land and light and people and revealing survival and beauty, he reminds us that the Caribbean should not be a place that is an idyll or a nightmare but rather a place where people live, work, and endure.[7]

Notes

Introduction

1 Sidney Mintz, *Sweetness and Power: The Place of Sugar in Modern History* (New York: Penguin, 1985), pp. xv–xvi.

2 Economic Commission for Latin America and the Caribbean, *Statistical Yearbook for Latin America and the Caribbean, 2006*, <http://website.eclac.cl/anuario_estadistico/anuario_2006/eng/index.asp>, accessed 30 March 2007.

1 Transporting citizenship

1 Michel-Rolph Trouillot, *Haiti: State against Nation: The Origins and Legacy of Duvalierism* (New York: Monthly Review Press, 1990).

2 Nina Glick Schiller and Georges Eugene Fouron, *Georges Woke up Laughing: Long Distance Nationalism and the Search for Home* (Durham, NC: Duke University Press, 2001), p. 201.

3 Opitz Gotz-Dietrich, "Transnational organizing and the Haitian crisis, 1991–1994", *Journal of Haitian Studies*, 8(2) (2002): 114–26.

4 The best account of this is Jonathan Demme's 2004 documentary, *The Agronomist*.

5 François Pierre-Louis, "Can hometown associations foster democratic change in Haiti?", *Journal of Haitian Studies*, 8(2) (Fall 2002): 127–45; Francois Pierre-Louis, "Democracy, civil society, and the hometown associations", *Wadabagei*, 5(2) (2002): 49–76.

6 Alex Dupuy, "Globalization, the World Bank, and the Haitian economy", in Franklin W. Knight and Teresita Martínez-Vergne (eds), *Contemporary Caribbean Cultures and Societies in a Global Context* (Chapel Hill: University of North Carolina Press, 2005).

7 Dennis A. V. Brown, "Inbetweenity: marginalization, migration and poverty among Haitians in the Turks and Caicos Islands", in Sandra Courtman (ed.), *Beyond the Blood, the Beach and the Banana: New Perspectives in Caribbean Studies* (Kingston, Jamaica: Ian Randle, 2004).

2 Sell it to save it

1 Marifeli Pérez-Stable, *The Cuban Revolution: Origin, Course, and Legacy* (New York: Oxford University Press, 1993); Susan Eva Eckstein, *Back from the Future: Cuba under Castro* (New York: Routledge, 2003), 2nd edn.

2 "Gorbachev–Castro face-off: a clash of styles and policies", *New York Times*, 2 April 1989; "Gorbachev begins his visit to Cuba with Castro's hug",

8 Carl Stone, "Hard drug use in a black island society: a survey of drug use in Jamaica", *Caribbean Studies*, 24(3–4), 1991: 267–88.

9 Barry Chevannes, Webster Edwards, Anthony Freckleton, Norma Linton, DiMario McDowell, Aileen Standard-Goldson, Barbara Smith, "A report of the National Commission on Ganja to Rt Honorable P. J. Patterson, QC, MP, Prime Minister of Jamaica", 7 August 2001.

10 Duane Blake, *The Shower Posse: The Most Notorious Jamaican Crime Organization* (New York: Acorn Alliance, 2003).

4 Wired on the islands

1 Daniel Miller and Don Slater, *The Internet: An Ethnographic Approach* (New York: Berg Publishers, 2000).

2 John Coté, "Cubans log on behind Castro's back", in Lydia Chávez (ed.), *Capitalism, God, and a Good Cigar: Cuba Enters the Twenty-first Century* (Durham, NC: Duke University Press, 2005).

3 Carla Freeman, *High Tech and High Heels in the Global Economy: Women, Work, and Pink-collar Identities in the Caribbean* (Durham, NC: Duke University Press, 2000).

4 Carla Freeman, "Is local:global as feminine:masculine? Rethinking the gender of globalization", *Signs*, 26(4) (Summer, 2001): 1007–37.

5 Antiguan prime minister Baldwin Spenser, cited in "PM to US: Withdraw WTO appeal", *Antigua Sun*, 17 January 2005.

6 "US claims victory on Web betting ban; others see WTO ruling as murky", *The Washington Post*, 8 April 2005.

Conclusion

1 Catherine A. Reinhardt, *Claims to Memory: Beyond Slavery and Emancipation in the French Caribbean* (New York: Berghahn Books, 2006).

2 Laurent Dubois, "History's quarrel: the future of the past in the French Caribbean", in Juanita de Barros, Audra Diptee and David V. Trotman (eds), *Beyond Fragmentation: Perspectives on Caribbean History* (Princeton, NJ: Marcus Wiener Publishers, 2006).

3 Michel-Rolph Trouillot, *Silencing the Past: Power and the Production of History* (Boston, MA: Beacon Press, 1995).

4 Jamaica Kincaid, *A Small Place* (New York: Farrar, Straus and Giroux, 1988).

5 *Jamaica Gleaner*, 18 February 2007.

6 Ibid., 12 December 2006.

7 Derek Walcott, "The Antilles: fragments of epic memory", Nobel Lecture, 1992, <http://nobelprize.org/nobel_prizes/literature/laureates/1992/walcott-lecture.html>.

Further reading

The conceptual underpinnings of this book were inspired by Sidney Mintz, *Sweetness and Power: The Place of Sugar in Modern History* (1985), Michel-Rolph Trouillot, *Silencing the Past: Power and the Production of History* (1995), Jamaica Kincaid, *A Small Place* (1988), and David Scott, *Conscripts of Modernity: The Tragedy of Colonial Enlightenment* (2004).

A classic general history of the Caribbean is Eric Williams, *From Columbus to Castro: The History of the Caribbean, 1492–1969* (1970); A more recent, extremely thorough history is the series edited by Bridget Brereton, *General History of the Caribbean*, vols I–VI.

For the histories and politics of the contemporary Caribbean see among others Denis Benn and Kenneth Hall, *Contending with Destiny: The Caribbean in the 21st Century* (2000), Franklin Knight, *The Caribbean: Genesis of a Fragmented Nationalism* (2nd edn, 1990), R. S. Hillman et al., *Understanding the Contemporary Caribbean* (2003), T. Skelton, *Introduction to the Pan-Caribbean* (2004), Robert Potter, David Barker, Dennis Conway and Thomas Klak, *The Contemporary Caribbean* (2004), Franklin Knight and Teresita Martínez-Vergne (eds), *Contemporary Caribbean Cultures and Societies in a Global Context* (2005), Thomas Klak (ed.), *Globalization and Neoliberalism: The Caribbean Context* (1998), Anthony Payne and Paul Sutton, *Modern Caribbean Politics* (1993), Sandra Courtman (ed.), *Beyond the Blood, the Beach, and the Banana: New Perspectives in Caribbean Studies* (2004). A collection that includes fascinating essays on Cuba and Colombia is Alma Guillermoprieto, *Looking for History* (2001).

On the United States and the Caribbean: Anthony Maingot, *The United States and the Caribbean* (1994) and Anthony Maingot and Wilfredo Lozano, *The United States and the Caribbean: Transforming Hegemony and Sovereignty* (2005).

A classic history of Haiti from the eighteenth to the twentieth century is David Nicholls, *From Dessalines to Duvalier: Race, Colour and National Independence in Haiti* (originally published in 1979, with editions in 1988 and 1996). On Haitians in the United States, see Alex Stepick, *Pride against Prejudice: Haitians in the United States* (1998), Nina Glick Schiller and Georges Eugene Fouron, *Georges Woke Up Laughing: Long-distance Nationalism and the Search for Home* (2001), Michael Laguerre, *Diasporic Citizenship: Haitian Americans in Transnational America* (1998). Recent accounts of Haitian political and economic change include Robert Rotberg (ed.), *Haiti Renewed: Political and Economic Prospects* (1997), Alex Dupuy, *Haiti in the New World Order: The Limits of the Democratic Revolution* (1997), Robert Fatton, *Haiti's Predatory Republic: The Unending Transition to Democracy* (2002). See also the autobiography by Jean-Bertrand Aristide, *Dignity* (1996).

The study of Caribbean migration is very extensive and diverse. Some general titles include Patricia Pessar, *Caribbean Circuits: New Directions in the Study of Caribbean Migration* (1996), Mary Chamberlain (ed.), *Caribbean Migration: Globalized Identities* (1998), Alejandro Portes and Josh Dewind, *Rethinking Migration: New Theoretical and Empirical Perspectives* (2007).

An excellent history of nineteenth- and twentieth-century Cuba is Louis A. Pérez Jr, *Cuba: Between Reform and Revolution* (1995). On the revolution in particular see Marifeli Pérez-Stable, *The Cuban Revolution: Origins, Course, and Legacy* (1993) and Susan Eckstein, *Back from the Future: Cuba under Castro* (2003). A comprehensive survey of the politics of health in revolutionary Cuba is Julie Feinsilver, *Healing the Masses: Cuban Health Politics at Home and Abroad* (1993). For the Special Period, see Eloise Linger and John Cotman, *Cuban Transitions at the Millennium* (2000), C. Peter Ripley, *Conversations with Cuba* (1996), Jorge F. Pérez-López, *Cuba at the Crossroads: Politics and Economics after the Fourth Party Congress* (1994), Lydia Chávez (ed.), *Capitalism, God, and a Good Cigar: Cuba Enters the Twenty-first Century* (2005).

Classic studies of Jamaica include Rex Nettleford (ed.), *Jamaica in Independence* (1989) and Anthony Payne, *Politics in Jamaica* (1988). On various aspects of the drug trade in Latin America and the Caribbean, see Coletta Youngers and Eileen Rosin (eds), *Drugs and Democracy in Latin America: The Impact of US Policy* (2005), Axel Klein, Marcus Day and Anthony Harriot (eds), *Caribbean Drugs: From Criminalization to Harm Reduction* (2004), Ron Chepesiuk, *Hard Target: The United States War against International Drug Trafficking, 1982–1997* (1999), Tom Farer (ed.), *Transnational Crime in the Americas* (1999); Ivelaw Griffith and Betty N. Sedoc-Dahlberg (eds), *Democracy and Human Rights in the Caribbean* (1997). A compelling if somewhat celebratory portrait of Marley and Rastafarian culture is Timothy White, *Catch a Fire: The Life of Bob Marley* (2000). Detailed narratives of drug trafficking and gang life are found in Laurie Gunst, *Born Fi' Dead: A Journey through the Jamaican Posse Underworld* (1995) and Geoff Small, *Ruthless: The Global Rise of the Yardies* (1995). A recent history of the rise and fall of cocaine in international contexts is Paul Gootenberg (ed.), *Cocaine: Global Histories* (1999).

A general account of communications technology and its impact in the region is Hopeton S. Dunn (ed.), *Globalization, Communications, and Caribbean Identity* (1995). See also essays in Ramesh Ramsaran (ed.), *Caribbean Survival and the Global Challenge* (2002), Jacqueline Anne Braveboy-Wagner and Dennis John Gayle (eds), *Caribbean Public Policy: Regional, Cultural and Socioeconomic Issues for the 21st Century* (1997). For labor and gender in Barbados, see the pathbreaking book by Carla Freeman, *High Tech and High Heels: Women, Work and Pink Collar Identities in the Caribbean* (2000). Gerald Sussman and John A. Lent (eds), *Global Productions: Labor in the Making of the "Information Society"* (1998), takes a global approach to the problem and includes essays on the Caribbean in particular. For an innovative approach to the study of information technologies see Daniel Miller and Don Slater, *The Internet: An Ethnographic Approach* (2000).

On history and memory in the Caribbean, see Juanita de Barros, Audra Diptee and David V. Trotman (eds), *Beyond Fragmentation: Perspectives on Caribbean History* (2006), Catherine A. Reinhardt, *Claims to Memory: Beyond Slavery and Emancipation in the French Caribbean* (2006), Pedro L. San Miguel, *The Imagined Island: History, Identity and Utopia in Hispaniola* (2005), Jeannette Allis Bastian, *Owning Memory: How a Caribbean Community Lost Its Archives and Found*

Its History (2003), Peter Hulme, *Remnants of Conquest: The Island Caribs and Their Visitors, 1877–1998* (2000), Maximilian C. Forte, *Ruins of Absence, Presence of Caribs: (Post)Colonial Representations of Aboriginality in Trinidad and Tobago* (2005).

Index